Str

Steven Denford

ISBN 0 904491 44 7

Staple Inn, photographed in 1938. The Inn, which was transferred from Camden to the City in 1994, is seen from the north side of Holborn, which remains in Camden. The half-timbering is a 20th-century restoration, but this is how most of the buildings lining this street would have looked in the 16th century.

Streets of Old Holborn

Compiled by   Steven Denford and David Hellings
with major contributions by
David and Ruth Hayes

Edited by   F Peter Woodford

Designed by   Ivor Kamlish

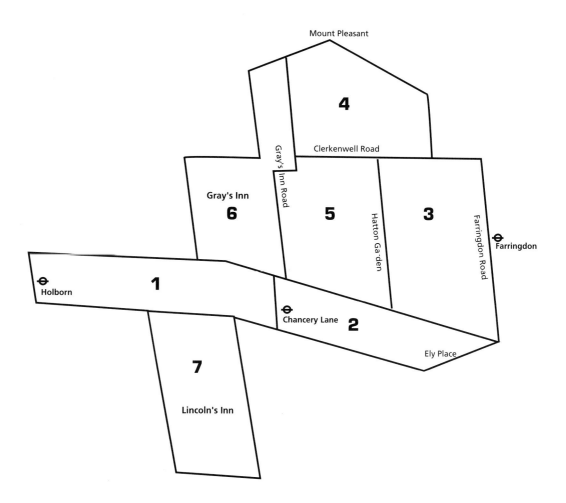

Mount Pleasant

4

Clerkenwell Road

Gray's Inn Road

Gray's Inn

6

5

Hatton Garden

3

Farringdon Road

⊖ Farringdon

⊖
Holborn

1

⊖ Chancery Lane

2

Ely Place

7

Lincoln's Inn

Contents

Acknowledgements

The research and text of most of this book were the work of Steven Denford and David Hellings, but major contributions were made by Ruth and David Hayes, particularly in the section on Little Italy; David Hayes also provided the information and illustrations on boundary changes (p 8) and on the Liberties (p 13).

For the early history of the parish we have drawn heavily on Caroline M Barron's admirable *The parish of St Andrew Holborn*, to which we owe a particular debt of gratitude. The librarians of Gray's Inn and Lincoln's Inn, respectively Theresa Thorn and Guy Holborn, were kind enough to check and correct the passages on those Inns. Our other sources of information are listed on p 83.

Most of the illustrations were supplied by the unfailing resource of the Camden Local Studies and Archive Centre. The National Monuments Record (now part of English Heritage) and the Pearl Assurance Archive also provided and/or gave permission to reproduce Figs 1–5, 16, 23 and 24. The sketch map on the back cover by Ivor Kamlish was based on Ordnance Survey maps of 1914, adapted to reflect subsequent change.

A note on typeface codes

Buildings named or numbered in the text in bold type were extant at the time of writing (February 1999); those in plain roman type were no longer in being.

F Peter Woodford

Illustrations

A note on boundaries

Since the local government boundaries relevant to this book were changed (a) with the introduction of Metropolitan Boroughs in 1899, (b) with the formation of the amalgamated London Boroughs in 1965 and (c) again in 1994, David Hayes and Ivor Kamlish have provided three maps (p 9) for the reader's assistance.

The historic Middlesex parish of St Andrew Holborn stretched from the river Fleet, its natural eastern boundary, westward to the borders of the manor of Bloomsbury (present day Southampton Row) and St Giles-in-the-Fields. By the early medieval period the City of London had extended its boundaries across the Fleet as far as Holborn Bars (p 10), embracing the south-eastern corner of Holborn parish, and with it the parish church of St Andrew. As followers of Route 2 in particular will become aware, present-day Holborn (the street) is divided between the London Borough of Camden and the City of London.

Before 1899 the situation was far more complex, as Map 1 illustrates. St Andrew's parish had for centuries comprised three Liberties, functioning for all non-spiritual purposes as independent parishes (see p 13). The portion of Holborn lying within the City of London was known popularly as the *City Liberty*, and officially as the Parish of St Andrew Holborn London. Outside the City boundary, Holborn was divided between two further Liberties. Its western reaches comprised the *Liberty above the Bars*, also named the Parish of St Andrew Holborn Middlesex; while its north-eastern corner was known variously as the *Upper Liberty* and as the *Liberty of Saffron Hill, Hatton Garden and Ely Rents*.

Also shown in Map 1 are Holborn's Inns of Court and Inns of Chancery (see p 15), which were 'extra-parochial' enclaves, outside the jurisdiction even of the Liberties in which they lay; and Ely Place, whose very special status is described on p 14.

In 1723, the ecclesiastical parish of St George the Martyr was created, to serve a newly built-up area west of Red Lion Street; but the old western Liberty remained intact for civil purposes as the 'United Parishes of St Andrew above Bars and St George the Martyr'.

In 1899 the Saffron Hill Liberty and the United Parishes, together with their enclaves, joined with two westerly parishes to form 'Holborn', the smallest of the Metropolitan Boroughs (Map 2). This, in turn, merged in 1965 with Hampstead and St Pancras as part of the London Borough of Camden.

Boundary changes in 1994 rationalised the age-old irregular western borders of the City of London. In the process, Camden *gained* (from Westminster) both Chichester Rents (p 82) and part of Carey Street (p 81). It also won sole jurisdiction over the north side of Holborn (the street), through which the City boundary had previously cut like a jigsaw, see Map 2 (for a possible explanation of the jaggedness of this boundary, see p 14). Camden *lost* the north-east end of Chancery Lane, with its offshoot Quality Court, together with Southampton Buildings, on the site of former Southampton House (seat of the Wriothesley Earls of Southampton) and, on the south side of Holborn, Staple Inn. This building is so spectacular (see frontispiece), and so typical of what the street used to look like in the 16th century, that we mention it briefly (p 26) even though since 1994 it has been out of our area.

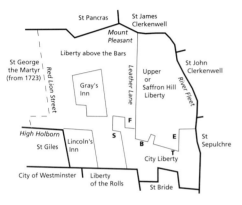

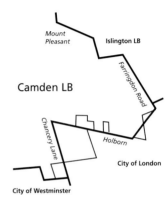

Map 1
St Andrew Holborn before 1899, with its Liberties and their extra-parochial enclaves (B, Barnard's Inn; E, Ely Place; F, Furnival's Inn; S, Staple Inn; T, Thavies Inn).

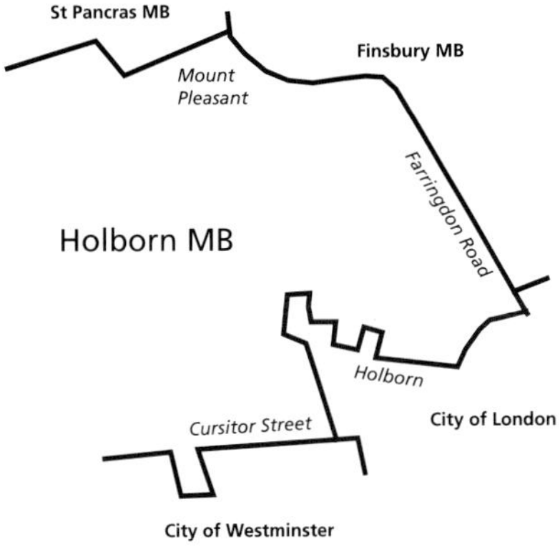

Map 2
Boundaries, 1899–1964.

Map 3
Boundaries since 1994; feint lines show the 1965–94 Camden boundary.

9

Historical overview

Holborn is an area steeped in history, having multitudinous associations with monarchs and courtiers and the rich and famous as well as with the poor and unknown. Until the early 1700s this was the edge of London, and although the area is now bounded by Victorian thoroughfares (such as Farringdon Road, Clerkenwell Road, and Charterhouse Street) which dramatically altered traffic circulation, much of the layout of the small streets in between is unchanged.

The street **HOLBORN** (now *High Holborn* for the part that lies west of Gray's Inn Road) follows the line of the Roman road from Londinium that joined up with the road from the stronghold at Colchester to the west of England. This road was actually made before Londinium was founded in AD 50; it lay to the north of Londinium's future site. At Tyburn, present-day Marble Arch, it met Watling Street, a strategic Roman road from the Kent coast to northern Britain, which crossed the Thames at what was to become Westminster. Londinium was founded downstream of this, where the Thames was narrow enough to be bridged (perhaps as late as AD 100) yet deep enough to carry maritime traffic. Thereafter, traffic through Londinium made use of the east–west road for all overland transport both to the west (Brentford and Staines) and to the north-west (Verulamium and Chester). These latter destinations were reached by taking a sharp right turn at Tyburn up northbound Watling Street. Building a road directly from Londinium to the north-west would have meant going straight over Hampstead Hill, a climb of over 400 feet – no small challenge for the wagons of the day. It was around the axis of this east–west road that the later village and borough of Holborn were to grow.

Little happened by way of settlement here for the next 1000 years. Some Roman remains (coins and funerary items) have been found in the vicinity, but little evidence of habitation. In the 10th century the westbound road was still a wide army street; in 959 King Edgar the Peaceable granted land south of the street, including the old wooden church of St Andrew at Holebourne, to Westminster Abbey. The name Holborn comes from the *bourne in the hollow*, in other words the steep-sided valley of the River Fleet, which here forms the eastern boundary of Camden just as in former times it formed the eastern boundary of the parish of St Pancras (north of our area) and, further south, that of the parish of St Andrew, Holborn. Most of the original village of Holebourne lay to the east of present-day High Holborn, near to the City.

Domesday Book contains a cryptic reference to two cottagers at Holebourne who paid 20d a year (not an enormous sum, even by the values of the day) to the king's sheriff, but we can only speculate as to their location and status. Light begins to break through only in the reign of Henry II (1154–1189), when William Fitzstephen described Holborn as an area of fields and pasture land where young men practised the martial arts (leaping, archery, wrestling, stone and javelin throwing) and, even at this early date, football. By this time the boundaries of the City of London had crept out from the original Roman walls, and the City ward of Farringdon Without took in a substantial proportion of the parish of St Andrew's, including the parish church. The Holborn Bars were set up at the City boundary to regulate entry and exit and to exact tolls.

Early players in the development of the area were the Knights Templar (a crusading order founded soon after the capture of Jerusalem in 1099). They had a church on the south side of High Holborn as early as 1128, and probably laid down what is now Chancery Lane to link the Middle Temple with their church.

They were followed by ecclesiastics. At a time when the church was virtually the sole repository of education and administrative expertise, bishops were major figures of state, and the more important of them needed a London base from which to influence the counsels of the king. The bishops of Lincoln established themselves in and around the Templars' church when that church moved elsewhere. The bishops of remote Bangor had a place in Shoe Lane. More significantly, the powerful bishops of Chichester and Ely built London 'palaces' in Chancery Lane and what is now Ely Place respectively.

By this time (the late 13th century) Holborn was beginning to take shape. 'Holeburnstreete' itself is first mentioned in 1249, and lanes running north from it began to appear soon after. Portpoole Lane (later Gray's Inn Lane, now Road) led north to the manor, or Soke, of Portpoole, and Lyvereslane (now Leather Lane) and Goldineline (later Field Lane, and Saffron Hill) are mentioned in the 1290s. The basic street pattern east of Gray's Inn Road and Chancery Lane seems to have been established by 1300. Holborn itself was, as it had been in Roman times, a major highway, carrying wool, hides, corn, cheese and wood into the City. This presumably accounts for the amazing number of taverns in the area: 25 outside the City limits in Holborn alone are recorded in 1384, and a staggering 75 in the ward of Farringdon Without. In 1417 Holborn was paved by order of King Henry V, though probably at that stage only as far west as the boundary of the City.

After the ecclesiastics came the lawyers.

(For the origins of the Inns of Court, see p 15.) It was natural for the fledgling legal profession to establish itself on virgin land that was not only clear of the City – giving lawyers the space they needed to build their halls, chapels, chambers and gardens – but handy for the king's courts at Westminster. By the beginning of the 15th century the four major inns and their satellite inns of chancery were well established. Two of the major inns, namely Lincoln's Inn and Gray's Inn, lie within the present-day borough of Camden, though only one of the inns of chancery (Furnival's, now demolished) once did so; surviving Staple Inn was claimed in 1994 by the City.

Development in plague-struck late medieval London was slow, and it was not until another 100 years or more had passed that ordinary houses began to appear beyond the western limits of the City. The process seems to have been unregulated, and went largely unrecorded. The parish of St Andrew's never included major estates such as those which defined the development of much of Camden, and there was no proper manor (what there was consisted only of a few messuages – properties with adjoining land – and gardens squeezed between Shoe Lane and the Fleet). By the second half of the 16th century ribbon development extended along High Holborn as far as the site of modern Kingsway and for several hundred

yards up the east side of what was then Gray's Inn Lane. An Act of 1542 ordered that Holborn be paved as far as the village of St Giles. But there were still green fields between Holborn and St Giles, and the Bishop of Ely's palace was almost in open country.

This early (16th-century) development seems to have been mainly of good houses for wealthy, or relatively wealthy, Londoners wishing to escape the confines of the City. But Holborn never became a smart residential suburb. This was due partly to the rival attractions of the Strand (closer to Westminster and the river) and partly to the fact that as a major highway Holborn must have attracted service industries (taverns, stables, farriers) that would have interfered considerably with the peace and open space which its residents presumably sought. Gradually commerce took over, and by 1720 Strype was describing Holborn as "very spacious, well built and inhabited by tradesmen, as being a place of so great resort for stage coaches and wagons, as also by gentry and others that come to town, induced thereof from the accommodations of several inns."

For the same reasons, the Holborn area was never much favoured for the houses of the great, as was to be the case further west. There were a few, generally short-lived, exceptions. The Earl of Southampton bought the Bishop of Lincoln's town house on the east corner of Holborn and Chancery Lane (and thus just outside our area) in 1547, but his successors were never enthusiastic about it and petitioned for permission to pull it down and redevelop the land, which was finally done in 1650. The Earl of Warwick built Warwick House on the site of present First Avenue House immediately after the Civil War, but it lasted little more than 50 years before it was demolished. Bath Place, the London home of the Earls of Bath, lasted a little longer. Built around 1540 on the site of present Brooke Street, it was remodelled by Fulke Greville (1st Baron Brooke) and renamed Brooke House in the 1620s, and demolished shortly after 1676.

Perhaps the most important 'great house' in the area was that built by Sir Christopher Hatton, favourite of Elizabeth I, on grounds effectively extorted from the Bishop of Ely (p 35). But this house too proved short-lived. Under the Commonwealth, Hatton's successors pulled it down and began to develop the estate Sir Christopher had acquired into a consciously up-market district. What is now Hatton Garden and its adjoining streets became an oasis of gentility (see the illustration on p 13) in an area which otherwise developed piecemeal and much of which rapidly became notorious for vice and crime.

If the 16th century was a period of ribbon development along Holborn and Gray's Inn and Chancery Lanes, the 17th century was the period when, despite constant and unavailing efforts by the authorities to restrict the growth of London, the area filled out, the process being accelerated after 1666 by refugees from the Great Fire. We have already noted the development of the Hatton estate in the1650s, which was accompanied (or perhaps preceded) by unregulated infilling of the area between Ely Place and the Fleet. In the 1630s came the development of Lincoln's Inn Fields (in the parish of St Giles-in-the-Fields, to be covered in a future publication), and in the 1680s development spread to the north of Holborn around Red Lion Square. By the time Strype updated Stow's Survey in 1720 (see p 83), High Holborn had become part of London.

The area with which we are concerned enjoyed mixed fortunes in the 18th and 19th centuries. High Holborn itself, and most of the courts and alleys radiating off it, became solidly commercial: a mass of shops and small businesses, many of them connected with the printing and publishing industries, interspersed with lawyers and, later, accountants and architects, together with many taverns and hotels. The Inns of Court no doubt helped attract professional people. The area around Hatton Garden remained genteel until it too was largely taken over by commerce. But in the area down by the Fleet, and in the warren of little courts and alleys between Leather Lane and Gray's Inn Road, things were very different. The Bishops of Ely had already begun to let off parts of the palace grounds in the 17th century. As an inheritance from the right of sanctuary that had existed when the Bishops held sway, the whole of the land from Leather Lane to the Fleet and as far north as 'Hockley-in-the-Hole' (present Ray Street) was created a Liberty (see the note on Liberties, below). Policing arrangements here were weak, and by the 18th century local slums were as notorious for criminality as any in London. In the second half of the 19th century major efforts were made to clear them with the widening of Gray's Inn Road and the construction of Holborn Viaduct, Farringdon Road, Charterhouse Street, Clerkenwell Road and Rosebery Avenue.

The half-century before World War I saw further major changes, with the development of Hatton Garden into a centre for the diamond trade and the arrival of the big insurance companies (the Prudential and the Pearl) whose huge, deliberately ostentatious buildings initially dwarfed the small businesses surrounding them. The trend has continued since, hastened by the severe damage Holborn received during World War II. Since the war, much of our area has been covered by the mammoth glass and concrete blocks that typify modern commercial architecture. Whether this trend will

continue remains to be seen: it has been
abruptly checked by the slump in
construction of new office buildings and
increased public sensitivity to
environmental values. Meanwhile, despite
the ravages of the Luftwaffe and the
developers, there remains much to see and
enjoy. We hope this book will bring to the
reader some hitherto hidden treasures.

A note on Liberties

The right of sanctuary, whereby a criminal
or one accused of crime could escape the
law for a while by taking refuge in a church
or on Church property (e.g. a monastery,
abbey, or episcopal palace grounds), was
considered sacrosanct in the middle ages.
When Church land became the property of
others for building purposes, the right was
often preserved in the creation of a Liberty,
a district only loosely under the jurisdiction
of local justices of the peace or manorial
courts. The rights of sanctuary in Liberties
ended in 1623 for criminals and for civil
offenders through legislation in 1697 and
1723, but their independence from 'outside
interference', in particular by officers of the
parish in which they lay, continued.

By the 16th century, the parish of St
Andrew Holborn, whose medieval role as
a home to bishops has already been noted
(p 11), consisted entirely of three such
Liberties. Although their inhabitants

*The long-
demolished
Victorian
doorway of
No. 41/42
Hatton
Garden, in
a real mish-
mash of
classical
styles,
reflecting the
wealth and
not always
well-informed
pretension of
houses in
Hatton
Garden from
the 17th to
the late 19th
century.*

shared a single parish church for worship, each Liberty functioned for civil purposes as an autonomous parish within a parish. Each was governed by a 'Vestry', appointed its own officers and levied its own rates (chiefly for the purpose of relieving the poor within its boundaries). Such arrangements persisted, with some variations, until the formation of the borough of Holborn in 1899.

The City Liberty occupied that part of the parish lying within the City of London (i.e., in the Ward of Farringdon Without). Westward and north-westward, in the County of Middlesex, lay the Liberty above the Bars. Also in Middlesex, to the east between Leather Lane and the Fleet, lay the Upper Liberty or Liberty of Saffron Hill, Hatton Garden and Ely Rents, an area once occupied by the grounds of Ely Palace (p 34).

During the Middle Ages, the part of modern Cambridgeshire known as the Isle of Ely was subject to the authority of the Bishops of Ely. When the bishops established their London base in Holborn in the late 13th century, they secured the agreement of the Crown to treat their palace similarly. This, and its grounds, were thus exempt from the jurisdiction of both the king's sheriff and the local Church hierarchy. In the 16th century, the bishops lost much of their London property to the Hatton family (see p 35). In 1772, they sold to the Crown what remained of their

land, by then amounting to little more than the present Ely Place and adjoining Mitre Court. After these were built in 1773, their inhabitants claimed independence from the adjacent Liberty of Saffron Hill (etc.), as occupants both of Crown land and of what they alleged to be still part of the See of Ely (and thus part of what had now become Cambridgeshire). The licensing and opening hours of the Mitre tavern (p 37) long remained under the control of the Cambridgeshire justices, and the (claimed) exemption of Ely Place residents from payment of the Liberty poor rate was ended only in 1835. In other respects Place and Court continued to enjoy a special status. The Ely Place Improvements Act of 1842 provided for its government by elected commissioners with powers to levy rates and see to the "paving, lighting, watching, cleaning and improving" of the area. This arrangement lasted until 1901, when most of the powers of the commissioners were transferred to Holborn Borough Council. But the Act is still on the statute book, the commissioners continue to meet, and Ely Place remains one of the last private roads in Inner London.

The creation of Liberties may explain the curiously jagged pattern of the City boundary on the north side of Holborn until 1994, shown in Maps 1 & 2 on p 9. The medieval boundary may have run neatly behind the houses on this north

side before the Liberty of Saffron Hill, Hatton Garden and Ely Rents cut into it from the north. Commercial premises (shops, inns, etc), however, remained under City jurisdiction, and it is their 'footprints' that form the northward wiggles on the pre-1994 map. As an Inn of Chancery, Furnival's Inn was, like a Liberty, exempt from the City's control. By the 19th century, however, it lay half outside and half within the City: its earliest building was set back from the street but the Holborn frontage, being lined with shops, stayed in the City. When the shops were later demolished, and the Inn extended out to the street, the City boundary remained unchanged.

Historical note
on the Inns of Court

The precise origins of the Inns of Court are lost in the mists of time. Being purely voluntary organisations, unchartered and unincorporated, they had no definite beginning, and at first left no records. But it is possible to surmise something of their history from the facts that are known about the legal system in medieval England.

By the 13th century, that system had developed to a form which would be recognisable today. The common law was well established, the king's courts sat at Westminster presided over by judges the king had appointed, and the king's judges also journeyed through the country holding assizes, which may be seen as the predecessors of the modern crown and county courts.

The development of the royal courts led naturally to the development of a class of professional pleaders in those courts, from whose ranks the judges were selected. These pleaders were at first completely unregulated, and the need quickly arose for a proper system of education and qualification. Such a system could not be provided by the universities: they were designed to train clerks for holy orders, and persons in holy orders were prohibited from pleading in secular courts even had they been qualified to do so (it was to be a matter of considerable importance in the development of English common law that it was free from clerical control). Instead, a rough and ready system of apprenticeship grew up in which those ambitious for a legal career attached themselves to those already learned in the law. But this system was inadequate to cope with the growing amount of legal business, and there was a clear need to put legal training on a more formal basis.

It is tempting to see the origin of the Inns of Court in a proclamation by Edward I in 1292 ordering that only those properly qualified could plead in the king's courts, and that such persons should be selected by the king's judges. As a result, it is argued, would-be pleaders grouped themselves together in fraternities where they could be taught by seasoned practitioners, and those fraternities developed into the Inns we know today. The theory may be close to the truth, but there is no direct evidence in support. In particular, there is little evidence that any of the inns existed, even in rudimentary form, as early as 1300. The foundation of Gray's Inn can be dated fairly precisely to around 1350 and the limited evidence suggests that the others were of similar age, though Lincoln's Inn may be older (see p 76 for the debate concerning its age). In any case, these early inns do not seem to have had any formal educational function; this emerged only in the 15th century.

However this may be, with the growth of legal business it was natural for practitioners and would-be practitioners of the law to gather in the London suburb nearest the courts at Westminster, and equally natural for them to come together in groups, perhaps in the house, or inn, of some senior lawyer or judge who could give them instruction, or just to share living expenses and experience.

Equally gradually, some of the inns began to acquire a reputation for learning which set them apart from the others. Thus arose the distinction between the four inns of court that have survived to the present day (Gray's and Lincoln's Inns, Inner and Middle Temple) and the 'inns of chancery' which in time took on the role of preparatory schools for the four major inns. The latter in the end largely took over one or more of the junior institutions by a process of formal affiliation (for example, Gray's Inn had formal links with Staple and Barnard's Inns).

It is not clear how the Inns of Chancery acquired their name. They had no particular connection with the Court of Chancery, which dealt with the overflow of civil litigation from the older courts of King's Bench and Common Pleas. One theory is that they were home, and possibly training ground, for the Chancery Clerks, who later migrated to Lincoln's Inn (see p 79). Alternatively, they may have taken their name simply from their proximity to Chancery Lane. In any event, by the middle of the 17th century they had lost their original function and ceased to be the main source of recruits for the four major inns; eventually they became little more than social clubs and providers of accommodation for solicitors, who were by definition excluded from the major inns. The last of them was sold off in 1903.

Quite early in the 15th century it became established that the king's *serjeants-at-law*, who alone could plead in the Court of Common Pleas and from whose ranks the judges were drawn, would be recruited only from the four Inns of Court. The inns developed their internal hierarchies and took on an increasingly formal educational role. By the 16th century they were effectively governed by a class of *readers*, barristers of sufficient seniority to have been chosen to give 'readings' or lectures. In addition, there was a category of *benchers* who sat on the bench during moots – then an important part of legal training – who might or might not be readers themselves. When the practice of giving readings declined the benchers became the governing bodies, as they are today. Below the readers came the *utter* or *outer barristers*, students of at least two or three years' seniority who had

been called to the bar of their Inn and sat outside the bar during moots. Below them in turn came the *inner barristers*, who were pupils not yet called to the bar and who sat within it.

There were some variations between individual inns: at Gray's Inn there was a fourth class of *ancients*, barristers of some seniority who had however not been appointed readers, while Lincoln's Inn and the Inner Temple were until the second half of the 16th century ruled by annually appointed governors.

It was not until the end of the 16th century that a call to the bar of an Inn conferred an automatic right of audience before the courts. Previously, that right was confined to barristers who had a certain seniority or who had been approved by the Chancellor or Chief Justice on the advice of the benchers. This effectively gave the benchers control over a young barrister's career. Right of audience at the Court of Common Pleas remained a monopoly of the serjeants-at-law until 1846.

The 16th and early 17th centuries were the great days of the Inns of Court. Many young men, Oliver Cromwell amongst them, joined them with no thought of a legal career but primarily for social reasons. For a person with no intention of entering holy orders they were an attractive alternative to the universities, and they became in effect a form of fashionable finishing school for the male gentry, many

of whom would go on to become justices of the peace and needed at least a smattering of knowledge of the law. The social side of the inns therefore also evolved, with elaborate masques and revels and occasional visits by royalty (pp 67,71,78). These revels were not just recreation. Singing, dancing and the playing of instruments were then part of the education of any young gentleman with pretensions to social standing and attendance at Court, and came by degrees to be included in the curriculum of the inns.

This golden age was brought to an abrupt end by the Civil War. Puritanism halted the masques and revels. The inns themselves split, many members joining the king's party, and the system of education, already in decline, was effectively suspended and never fully revived. By the 18th century the inns had become little more than social clubs, membership of which was compulsory if you wished to plead in the royal courts (the distinction between pleading barristers and non-pleading solicitors was by then well established). Qualification for the bar had come to depend on eating a certain number of dinners in hall and the recommendation of a judge or bencher, with the aspiring barrister left to fend for himself so far as education for his profession was concerned. Only in Victorian times did reform come with the establishment in 1852 of the Council of Legal Education (which became the Inns of Court School of Law in 1967). Even then, attendance at lectures was not compulsory, and it was not until 1872 that a compulsory examination for barristers replaced the previous system of patronage.

The Inns of Court flourish today as never before, and stand fully equal to the most ancient of our universities as a source of education and learning. Masques and revels are no longer part of the curriculum and pleadings are no longer made in Norman French, but if Thomas More (not the least famous alumnus of Lincoln's Inn) were to return today he would find much about the corporate life of the inns that was familiar even after nearly 500 years. The division into students, barristers and benchers remains, as does the requirement to eat a certain number of dinners in hall. The essential educational function of the inns has been restored, albeit in a form very different from that of More's day. The Inns of Court are a striking testimony to the continuity of the English legal tradition from its beginnings long ago in the Middle Ages.

Route 1
Along High Holborn from Kingsway to Gray's Inn Road

Leave Holborn Underground by the "High Holborn/British Museum" exit and pause to look around you, so far as the bustle of pedestrians and roar of traffic will permit. Behind us the Underground station (1906) is itself among the oldest buildings in sight, even though Holborn has been a busy commercial thoroughfare for at least three centuries. Permanent houses appeared in the first half of the 16th century, and the road is clearly visible on Agas's map of c.1560 as a snake of ribbon development stretching west from the city, paralleling the Strand to the south.

Like the Strand, though on a far more modest scale, Holborn seems to have been at first a residential development for those seeking to escape the confines of the City. For perhaps 100 years it stood alone, with green fields on either side. Only in the second quarter of the 17th century, with the development of Covent Garden and Lincoln's Inn Fields to the south, followed by Red Lion Square and the streets around it (in and after the 1680s) to the north, did Holborn become absorbed by London. It was never particularly fashionable, becoming instead a service area for the

developments to north and south.

By the 18th century Holborn was noted for its booksellers and allied trades (printers, publishers and engravers) and also as a notorious haunt for women of the town, who were supposed to be apprehended by the watch, but all too often escaped arrest by offering the watch their services for free. By the 19th century Holborn between Southampton Row and the City had become a miscellany of commercial enterprises and offices interspersed with a quite remarkable number of taverns (eighteen in the 1860s, plus four hotels) and several other places of entertainment. In the 20th century the character of the street has become almost wholly commercial. The small factories are long gone, the number of pubs has been reduced to five, and people no longer come to Holborn to be entertained.

The spot where we stand has long been a serious traffic bottleneck, in no way eased by a planning mistake of the 1890s which caused a new development on the north-west corner of what is now the Holborn–Kingsway crossing to be set too far forward, thereby sharply restricting the flow of westbound traffic. The construction of Kingsway between 1900 and 1905 did little to alleviate the situation. There were proposals for a flyover as early as 1929. No action was taken, however, until the early 1960s, when Procter Street was cut through from Theobalds Road and the

present one-way system was created.

Look across the road to the blue plaque on the Cheltenham & Gloucester building on the corner of Southampton Row. This commemorates Thomas Earnshaw, who perfected the marine chronometer; his workshop stood on this site (**No.119**) for some 50 years. Although credit for inventing the chronometer has rightly gone to John Harrison, his invention was too expensive to be an economic proposition for every ship, and it was Thomas Earnshaw who simplified the mechanism and shortened the time of manufacture, bringing the price down to the point where every ship's captain could afford one. He was awarded £3000 in 1805 by the Board of Longitude in recognition of his achievements.

Spare a glance also for **Nos.114–5** on the north side, now another building society, built c.1900 and sporting fanciful carved panels – a light touch amid the unrelenting commercialism of much of modern High Holborn.

Turn left now and go a short distance down Kingsway before turning left again into **GATE STREET**. This marks the location of one of two gates on either side

1 Former grandeur up for sale: the façade of the blitzed Holborn Empire in 1951. (The advertisements for Tommy Trinder and the Andrews Sisters are of course for performances elsewhere.)

of High Holborn allowing James I and subsequent Stuart kings, and only the king and his courtiers, to cross that highway from the direction of Whitehall (via Drury Lane and Great Queen Street) to reach Theobalds Road on the way to their much-favoured hunting lodge at Theobalds in Hertfordshire. The first known houses in this short street dated from the 1630s, but nothing of them remains, and the street is now a gloomy canyon extensively decorated with graffiti and blocked by piles of rubbish. It is enlivened only at the far end by the **Ship Tavern**, rebuilt in 1923 but boasting of an ancestry going back to 1549. According to a tablet outside, it was once a haunt of recusants, and was frequented by Richard Penderel or Penderell (p 23) and the Chevalier d'Eon. This romantic character was often suspected of being a woman, because he adopted women's garb when he was engaged in spying activities, and indeed died in female attire.

After a short right turn, Gate Street debouches into Lincoln's Inn Fields (which is not covered in this book, being in the parish of St Giles-in-the-Fields), immediately before which on the left **WHETSTONE PARK** opens up. Now little more than an alley parallel to High Holborn, much of its north side was swallowed up by the Pearl Assurance development of 1912–14 (p 19). Whetstone Park was named after one

William Whetstone, who built it as a speculative development in the 1630s in defiance of the restrictions forbidding building beyond the City boundaries. His houses were ordered to be pulled down, but the order was not acted on and the street rapidly became known as a centre for vice and gambling. In 1682 the London apprentices, in a not infrequent outburst of moral fervour, descended on it and sacked the brothels. The watch were powerless to stop them and the apprentices clearly regarded the occasion as such a success that two nights later they returned and did it again. Whether this vigilante action was permanently successful is not recorded. Unlike High Holborn, Whetstone Park never developed commercially, and as late as 1900 appears to have been still largely residential.

Double back past the Ship, ignoring **LITTLE TURNSTILE** which runs alongside it, and turn right into **NEW TURNSTILE** to regain High Holborn. The three turnstiles (for Great Turnstile see p 22) were originally pedestrians' gates blocking the passage of sheep or cattle. At first this was *out of* Lincoln's Inn Fields into the highway, later *into* Lincoln's Inn Fields (when these had been lined with aristocratic houses) when any livestock were being driven along Holborn. Little and New Turnstiles are now mere alleyways, the former containing a few sandwich shops.

In High Holborn, pause to admire the confident inter-war building on your right at **No.233**, now occupied by the SEMA Group. This stands on the site of what was once an internationally known firm of bookbinders, the proprietors of which, a Mr and Mrs Tregaskis, were summoned to Windsor Castle in 1894 to show off their products to Queen Victoria. The present building was purpose-built in 1930 for Sir William Crawford to house his advertising agency, and is described by Pevsner as "a pioneer work in the history of modern architecture in England". Not everyone approved, and Crawford had to defend himself against charges that the building was 'teutonic'. Next door is an elegant *art deco* building whose ground floor is now occupied by the Woolwich building society.

After a few more shops we come to a huge block (Nos.247-261) currently being converted into the Chancery Court Hotel. On part of this site formerly stood the much-loved Holborn Empire music-hall (Fig 1). There is little in High Holborn today to offer relief from the stern imperatives of commerce, but between the wars this section of High Holborn was a centre of London night-life: besides the Empire, the well-known Holborn Restaurant was nearby, just west of Kingsway at No.218, and the Holborn Stadium Club was nearly opposite, on the site of post-WW II **Templar House**. The Club was built as a stadium for equestrian

entertainments in 1867 and went through various uses, ending up as a centre for wrestling and boxing competitions. The Holborn Empire was built in 1858 by one Edward Weston on the site of a nonconformist chapel. Originally known simply as Weston's Music Hall, it acquired the grander name about 1900. Its high point was, perhaps, Sybil Thorndike's Hecuba in *The Trojan Women* in 1930; others who appeared included Marie Lloyd and George Robey. The theatre closed in 1939 and was badly damaged in the blitz. It never reopened, though for 15 years after the war the bombed façade remained as a bleak memorial.

Next door on the redevelopment site is the shell of the Pearl Assurance building. Built in 1912–14 by Percy Moncton in the best Edwardian high baroque style (Fig 2, p 20), the Pearl Assurance was High Holborn's most distinctive and perhaps also most distinguished building. No expense was spared in the construction of what was to be the headquarters of Britain's second largest life assurance company, and the ground floor included marble floors, columns and tiling. The building was extended in 1932, 1957 and finally into the site of the Holborn Empire in 1960–62. But it was already becoming out of date, and incapable of coping with growing consumer demand and the modern technology that went with it. In 1990 the company moved out to

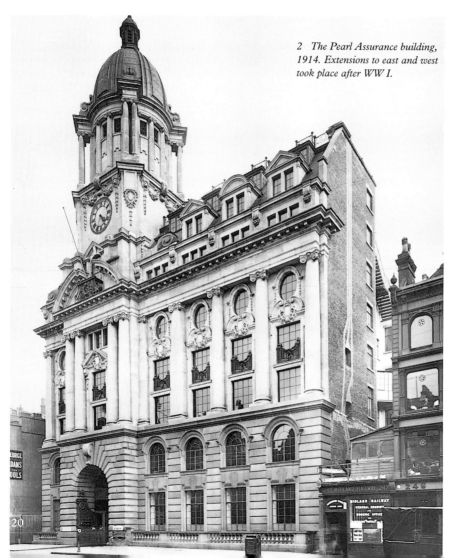

2 *The Pearl Assurance building, 1914. Extensions to east and west took place after WW I.*

Peterborough, and after various wrangles over planning permission it is now being converted into a hotel, though the façade is being retained.

The buildings that the Pearl building replaced (Nos.249–252) are to be seen in Fig 3, which shows the same Midland Railway booking office as in Fig 2 and also a shop which even at this early date (c.1905) was offering nicotine-free cigarettes and cigars for sale.

Much of the north side of High Holborn suffered greatly in the blitz. One survivor is **Turnstile House** at Nos.94–99. Built in 1937 in comparatively restrained 1930s monumental style, the top floors sport unexpected Corinthian capitals and other classical motifs. In the 1890s businesses on the site included Batsford's the booksellers and Edwards' *Harlene* hair restorer, which shamelessly promised to cure baldness (there was no Advertising Standards Authority in those days). Earlier still it had been the site of a blacking factory whose proprietor, Charles Day, was blind. He died in 1836 and founded an institute for the blind (*not* the Royal National Institute for the Blind, which was founded only in 1868) with a bequest of £100,000. Day's charity was administered by the Clothworkers' Company, and seems to have been mainly involved in paying pensions to indigent persons who had lost their sight.

Further along the south side of High

Holborn, at No.70, once stood the George and Blue Boar inn, one of the taverns where condemned men on their way to the gallows at Tyburn could take a glass of refreshment. Swift wrote:

As Clever Tom Clinch, while the rabble was
bawling
Rode stately through Holborn to die in his calling
He stopt at The George for a bottle of sack
And promised to pay for it when he came back.

The inn was a major centre for the coaching trade, and is recorded as having stabling for no fewer than 52 horses in 1779. But the development of railways rendered coaching inns obsolete, and in 1864 it was pulled down and replaced, logically enough, by a hotel to cater for those who now came to London by train. The Inns of Court Hotel no doubt sought to attract visitors with legal business at the nearby Gray's and Lincoln's Inns. The hotel lasted until 1923, when in turn was pulled down and a branch of Montague Burton arose on the site. Converted into a telephone exchange in 1929, it now houses the British Telecom archive and sits above the Kingsway trunk exchange – a small underground city of electrical and electronic equipment through which a major proportion of London's long-distance telephone calls are routed.

At Nos.73–78 on the north side stands **Hanover House**, another survivor of the blitz, dating from the end of the 1920s.

3   Nos.244–252 High Holborn in 1905: Nos. 249–252 were the first to be replaced by the Pearl Assurance building (Fig 2). Note the Midland railway ticket agency (still there in 1914, see Fig 2) and the advertisements in a 3rd-floor window for non-nicotine cigars and cigarettes.

It makes an interesting contrast with No.233 (p 20), of almost the same date. A further survivor, on the corner of Red Lion Street, is the **Old Red Lion** public house. It was here that the bodies of Oliver Cromwell, his son-in-law Henry Ireton and John Bradshaw, the president of the commission which tried Charles I, were taken after they had been disinterred following the Restoration in 1660. After lying in the Red Lion overnight they were taken to Tyburn, hanged in public and then decapitated, the heads to be stuck on poles outside Westminster Hall. It is recorded that although all three bodies had been embalmed, Bradshaw's embalming had not been successful and his body was badly decayed. One hopes that those who had to carry out this gruesome operation were well rewarded for their labours.

Beyond Red Lion Street there is at the time of writing a long void on the north side of the road. This is the site of State House, designed by Messrs Trehearne and Norman, Preston and Partners and completed in 1959. State House was regarded when it was built as the last word in prestige office development, a particular feature being the location of the main structural columns outside the building to increase flexibility inside; the forecourt boasted an abstract statue by Barbara Hepworth entitled *Meridian* and representing the free flow of the forces of nature (Fig 4). Alas for human aspirations,

within little more than 30 years of its first occupation the building was regarded as too out of date to be worth re-letting when the government departments renting it moved out, and it was demolished in 1993. The long delay in redeveloping the site (only in 1999 announced as to be Mid City Place) is apparently because office buildings are no longer built in London as speculations, as State House had been, and tenants have to be lined up in advance.

Next to the void is narrow **HAND COURT**, flanked by a grubby block of offices, empty at the time of writing, in the basement of which is the **Bung Hole** pub. A sign outside states that it was established in 1870, when Davy's the wine merchants, the current owners, was established; there has been a pub on the site for much longer than this. Known until the early 1900s as the Hand in Hand, it dates back at least to the 18th century and was for a time the headquarters of the Guild of Marriage Brokers (hence, perhaps, its name). After a period as the Irish House it was given its present name in 1970.

Reverting to the south side of the road, at **No.278** (now a hairdresser's) once stood the Russian Shop, a showcase for the arts and crafts of the Soviet Union. Opened at the height of the Cold War in 1961, it did not survive the collapse of communism and closed in 1990.

We come next to the third of the 'Turnstiles', namely **GREAT TURNSTILE**,

though it is narrow enough; cyclists are supposed to dismount, but don't. In late Georgian and Regency times, and indeed for many years afterwards, Great Turnstile was a major centre of the book trade. It still boasted two booksellers as late as the 1860s, not to mention a law stationer's, an engraver, a music seller and a numerical printer. At No.6, between 1799 and 1828, stood the offices of Luke Hansard, who began the systematic recording of the proceedings of Parliament; his son carried on the business from the same address until the 1850s. Nothing of the 19th century now survives in Great Turnstile, but the building on the corner of Lincoln's Inn Fields, **Dolphin Court**, is worth a glance as one of modern architecture's more successful products. Built in 1986, it sports a dolphin sculpture with the date 1989, and currently houses the Royal Commission on Local Government for England and Wales.

Beyond Great Turnstile, the whole of the ground floor of an otherwise undistinguished modern office block is occupied by the **Penderel's Oak** public house. The pub is a modern one, but the name commemorates the four Penderel brothers (so it should really be the "Penderels' Oak") who sheltered Charles II after his defeat at the Battle of Worcester in 1651. The 'oak' of course refers to the famous oak tree in which the king hid, and which was close to the Penderel brothers' house. After the Restoration the brothers came to London and were handsomely rewarded. One, Humphrey, lived for a while at No.19 Great Turnstile, while another, Richard, is recorded as an habitué of the Ship Inn in Gate Street (p 18) and is buried in the churchyard of St Giles.

On the same site stood until 1992 the London Weather Centre. Opened in Kingsway in 1959, it moved here in 1964 and was for over 30 years the public face of the Meteorological Office; one could drop in to pick up a weather forecast or find out more about how forecasts were prepared. But it seems to have been too expensive to survive the rigorous public-expenditure climate of the 1990s; in 1992 it closed its doors and moved to Clerkenwell Road (p 74), where it is not open to the public.

There is little in the remainder of the south side of High Holborn along to Chancery Lane that need detain us, though a Victorian building survives on the corner of Chancery Lane itself and the **Dutch House** at Nos.307–8 cheers us with its bright green panelling. Opened in 1962 as a showcase and exhibition of Dutch dairy products, it still houses the Netherlands–British Chamber of Commerce. Pause to admire on the north side the stolid classicism of **High Holborn House** at

4 Meridian, a 15-foot black bronze sculpture by Barbara Hepworth which stood in front of State House, 63–71 High Holborn, before its demolition. Present whereabouts unknown.

23

5 *First Avenue Hotel, 42–49 High Holborn, shortly after construction in 1884.*

Nos.52–54; built in 1930, the contrast with its near-contemporary buildings, Hanover House (p 21) and No.233 (p 19) is again striking.

East of High Holborn House the whole of the frontage between **BROWNLOW STREET** and Warwick Court, see below, is occupied by an early post-WW II development (1949–51), **First Avenue House**, Nos.42–49. Long occupied by various government departments – most notably, until 1997, the London bookshop of HMSO (now the Stationery Office) – it has recently been refurbished and now houses the Family Division of the Royal Courts of Justice (though High Court hearings are still held in the Strand). The site has had a chequered history. The Earl of Warwick, who had prudently sided with Parliament during the civil war, celebrated its successful conclusion by building Warwick House here in 1646. But Holborn never became a fashionable address for the aristocracy, and the building was demolished in 1708. The proprietor of a music shop at No.45, a Mr Bland, welcomed the composer Joseph Haydn on the latter's 1791 visit to London. Later a circus, subsequently converted into a theatre, arose, only to be burnt down in 1880. The opportunity was taken to clear the site and erect a prestigious late-Victorian development, the First Avenue Hotel. This was a no-expense-spared building in flamboyant Second Empire style (Fig 5) aimed at catering for the social élite. On the ground floor 'First Avenue Buildings' included a row of shops and for a time a post office. Sadly, the building suffered irreparable damage in the blitz and had to be pulled down; the present-day office block is a poor substitute.

Make a short detour into **WARWICK COURT**, where there is an Edwardian baroque survival at **Nos.4–5**. Further along on the right, pause to admire **No.8**. Owned by the benchers of Gray's Inn, the date *Gray's Inn 1697* proclaims its 17th-century origins, though it was extensively rebuilt in Regency times. Then, just before the archway leading to the Inns of Court School of Law in Gray's Inn (p 71) is a plaque topped by a portrait head of Sun Yat Sen (Sun Yixian, 1866–1925), described as the 'father of modern China', who led the first provisional government after the overthrow of the Chinese empire in 1911; he lodged here for a time when in exile.

Back in High Holborn, east of Warwick Court stands **Bracton House**, a surprisingly exotic 1980s building whose design appears to have been inspired by the *art deco* movement; opinions may differ as to whether this bold attempt at originality has been successful. At pavement level in its façade is a bronze sculpture by Eduardo Paolozzi entitled 'self portrait and strange machine'; apparently, the artist intended to depict himself as Hephaistos, god of fire and the working of metals.

After Bracton House we come to **FULWOOD PLACE**, which was a Tudor cart-track used as the south entrance to Gray's Inn until Sir George Fulwood acquired it, with some adjoining land, in 1580. He lined it with houses known as Fulwood's Rents and sold to Gray's Inn an even narrower entrance to the Inn's South Square that is still used today (see below). Strype mentions Fulwood Place as a likely spot for entertainment thanks to its proximity to Gray's Inn; at No.34 stood Squire's Coffee House (Fig 6). It was patronised by Addison, who received copy for *The Spectator* there.

Beyond Fulwood Place we encounter **Nos.31–33**. An otherwise unremarkable inter-war building, now known as Beck Greener House, it was for many years Chancery Lane Station Chambers, so called because the ground floor was occupied by Chancery Lane Underground station. The station moved across the road to a more convenient location on the Chancery Lane side in 1933.

Move on now to where a conspicuous clock announces the presence of the **Cittie of York** public house. A notice outside proclaims that a pub has stood on the site since 1430. This may be so, since Holborn was noted for its number of taverns as early as the 14th century, but from 1695 it was the premises of Henekey's, the wine merchants, who remained there until bought out in 1982. After a brief period as

6 *Squire's Coffeehouse in Fulwood's Rents (Fulwood Place), somewhat fancifully drawn in 1837.*

the Holborn Bar, the pub metamorphosed into the Cittie of York in 1986. The building we see now, despite its Tudor style, dates only from c.1900. The inside is worth inspecting: with its immense height and impressive wood ceiling, it has been compared to a baronial hall. The bar is one of the longest in Britain, and huge vats line the wall above it. Opposite are wooden cubicles that were originally installed so that lawyers from nearby Gray's and Lincoln's Inns could confer with their clients in privacy. The ancient iron stove in the middle, with three separate grates in Strawberry Hill gothic style, still works and is believed to be the one originally installed in the hall of Gray's Inn in 1815 (p 67).

Next to the Cittie of York stands a **gateway** to Gray's Inn. This was originally built in 1593 to provide a way into the Inn from High Holborn; the only entrance before this had been from Gray's Inn Road (Lane). The gate survived, albeit much rebuilt and latterly covered in Victorian stucco, until 1964, when it collapsed as a result of development work next door; what you see now is a modern replica.

Next to the Gray's Inn gateway, on the site of what is now Rymans the stationers, once stood the Grays Inn Coffee House, later the Grays Inn Hotel. Owned by the benchers of Gray's Inn, it dated back to the 17th century and had associations with Dickens: David Copperfield lodged there, and it is also mentioned in *The Old Curiosity Shop*. The site was redeveloped around 1870, and the hotel was replaced by a block of offices known as Gray's Inn Chambers, though a pub known initially as the Gray's Inn Tavern and from 1900 as the Irish House survived on the site until it was again redeveloped in the 1960s. It would appear that Irish 'theme pubs' with no particular connection with Ireland are not solely a modern phenomenon; confusingly, the old Hand in Hand at No.57 (p 22) was also renamed the Irish House at around the same time.

Only modern developments now stand

7A Middle Row, Holborn, pictured from the east. Note its proximity to half-timbered Staple Inn. It was demolished in 1867, leaving a very wide stretch of Holborn. See also p 27.

between us and Gray's Inn Road. Pause for a moment to glance across to where the road widens. This widening is due to the removal in 1867 of a group of houses known as Middle Row, which dated from the time when Holborn was first built up. It included from the 16th to the 19th century a "Quest House", where inquests on suspicious deaths occurring in the parish of St Andrew Above the Bars were held. Middle Row, which also included two of Holborn's many taverns, was regarded as a serious impediment to traffic as early as the 18th century (see Fig 7A, 7B), and it was eventually demolished, to general approval, by the Metropolitan Board of Works. The only problem was that this left the road too wide to be crossed safely, and the traffic island you see with its cast-iron pillar was accordingly erected in 1868; there is still a small plaque with the old Borough of Holborn coat of arms fixed to the lamp post at a slightly drunken angle.

You may now choose to enter the Chancery Lane Underground station (unless it is a Sunday) or continue with one of two walks in this book: Route 2 from here to Ely Place, or Route 6 around Gray's Inn (not on Saturday or Sunday).

7B Middle Row, Holborn, seen from the west in the 1830s.

27

The Prudential Building to Ely Place

Chancery Lane Tube station is closed on Sundays, so you may need to take a bus to our starting point, which is the junction of Holborn with Gray's Inn Road.

If you have come by Tube, emerge from Exit 2 of Chancery Lane station at the corner of Gray's Inn Road and walk east. From here along Holborn (no longer High Holborn) to Holborn Circus only the north side lies in Camden, the other side being in the City, so for this walk we shall concentrate our attention on the north side.

The two early-19th-century granite obelisks now topped with silver wyverns, erected in 1965 on either side of the road, mark the site of Holborn Bars, which were barriers (posts and chains) first erected in the 12th century to levy duties on traffic into the City, which lay to the east of the Bars.

As we look down the north side of **HOLBORN** towards the City it is hard to visualise the succession of taverns and coaching inns that once lined the street, such as the Greyhound, the Crown, the Chequer, the Bell and the Black Bull. In 1755 the street was described as "a place pestered with coaches which are a trouble to its inhabitants". Many Holborn inns remained in existence, some functioning as parcel, delivery and ticket offices long after the railways superseded coaches.

A visual impression of Old Holborn can be gained from the impressive black-and-white timber-framed building directly across the roadway, which since 1994 has ceased to be in Camden but which is impossible to ignore. This is Staple Inn (see frontispiece), one of the few remaining wooden buildings in the City. Its image used to grace the cover of 'Old Holborn' tobacco, once produced in a factory in Holborn Buildings, a court formerly leading off Holborn to the north behind us.

In the middle of the road stands the War Memorial of the Royal Fusiliers (City of London battalion) by Albert Toft, dated 1924. The soldier is modelled on a sergeant of the regiment and carries a rifle and kit; 22,000 Royal Fusiliers fell in WW I. The memorial, which also commemorates the dead of 1939–45, is used by the Royal Fusiliers on Remembrance Sunday.

We now begin walking towards the fiery red towering neo-Gothic edifice which was built (p 29) to house the Prudential Assurance Company. The first large block on the north side of Holborn (there are only three now, all the way to Holborn Circus) also belongs to the company, which developed **150 Holborn** in 1980 at a cost of £53 million, with banks and shops at ground level and 60,000 square feet of offices. The company employed its own architect, Gordon Collis, to oversee the design, which was intended to blend, at least as to colouring, with the older block next door. A building truly designed by the 'man from the Pru'!

The new block covers much of the west side of **BROOKE STREET**, which we now cross. The view up Brooke Street terminates in a 19th-century neo-Gothic building, with arched windows and green drainpipes, which is attached to the church of St Alban the Martyr (p 62). Brooke Street was formed after the demolition of palatial Brooke House in the late 17th century. In front of it was a large court, which covered the area where we are now standing. John Bourchier, created Earl of Bath in 1536, had inherited 3 acres of property on this side of Holborn, and built Bath Place, which became the earls' town residence. William Bourchier sold it in 1619 to Fulke Greville (1554–1628), who was made Lord Brooke in 1620, when he was Elizabeth I's Chancellor of the Exchequer; he was also a poet, intimate friend and biographer of Sir Philip Sydney and a patron of Ben Jonson and Shakespeare. The house was remodelled and renamed Brooke House. Here Greville was murdered by his manservant, a gentleman by birth, who had discovered his omission from Greville's will. He stabbed Greville and then stabbed himself.

Houses in Holborn were of great

architectural interest in early Stuart times – as seen in John Smythson's drawings on his visit in 1618, when he sketched the 'Holborn gable'. This was a gable with scrolled sides rising to a pediment, possibly inspired by Serlio and designed by Inigo Jones. Holborn gables were popular in the 1630s and 1640s, but vanished with the general adoption of the hipped roof and eaves under Charles II. Brooke House had a classically inspired cornice and seems to have been the earliest attempt at a classically fronted town house in London.

After Greville's death Brooke House passed to his kinsman Robert Greville. In 1656 representatives of the French Government were entertained here at Cromwell's expense and in 1668 the Brooke House committee, set up by Parliament to look into certain expenses of Charles II, met here. The house was demolished after Robert Greville's death in 1676 and disappears from maps in about 1680. The street was laid out soon after, and Strype in 1720 notes that building works had been completed with "new built houses, well inhabited".

Philip Yorke, Lord Chancellor from 1736 to 1756, was a clerk in chambers in Brooke Street, articled without a fee to an attorney for 3 years before moving to Lincoln's Inn. Thomas Chatterton, the poet, committed suicide at a house on the site of No.39 (then numbered No.4, on the west side near Holborn) by swallowing arsenic in water in 1770. He was 17 years old. He had tried to pass off his poems as the work of an undiscovered 15th-century poet called Thomas Rowley, but had failed to find a publisher. After his death he was hailed as a genius, Wordsworth describing him as "the Marvellous Boy". The morbid scene of his suicide is shown in the Pre-Raphaelite picture by Henry Wallis at the Tate.

In 1889 William Friese-Greene gave the first ever demonstration of 'moving pictures' at his laboratory at No.20. His reputation was at its height when he was immortalised in the film *The Magic Box*, starring Robert Donat and including every well-known British film star of the day, which was funded as part of the Festival of Britain in 1951. His tomb in Highgate Cemetery is inscribed "inventor of Kinematography" and bears the patent number (10301) of his invention, the kinematograph.

Having crossed Brooke Street we are standing by a City of London bollard dated 1991 (this side of Holborn has been wholly in Camden only since 1994). The corner of the **Prudential building** here was the earliest part of the building, erected in 1879 (although rebuilt in 1932 in a similar style), designed by Alfred Waterhouse. The Prudential Mutual Assurance, Investment and Loan Association was founded in 1848. It was initially aimed at the professional classes, but pressure from Parliament made it provide 'penny policies' to poorer workers so that they could save for their funerals.

The Company expanded with this business and changed its name to the Prudential Assurance Company. Needing larger offices, it moved here in 1879.

The 1879 building adjoined Furnival's Inn. This was an Inn of Chancery (p 15), founded in 1383 and taking its name from the Lords Furnival who had lived here. The Furnivals were said to have descended from one Fournyvals who rode to Palestine with Richard I. The Inn was first mentioned as a law seminary in 1409. Thomas More was a reader here for 3 years. By 1530 it was affiliated to Lincoln's Inn, which purchased the freehold of the Inn in 1547; thereafter, the Society of Furnival's Inn was the lessee. A grand front along Holborn was erected in the early 17th century, possibly to a design by Inigo Jones, but it was later neglected and derided when taste changed. By 1817 the Society had dwindled to 22 members, and Lincoln's Inn declined to renew its lease. The Society folded, and in 1818 a building lease was given to Henry Peto, uncle of his more famous later partner, Sir Samuel Morton Peto, who demolished the Inn but replaced it with a new building (Fig 8) bearing the same name.

In 1888 the Prudential paid Lincoln's Inn £150,000 for the freehold of Furnival's Inn, and demolished it in 1897 to allow for enlargement of their premises into what we see today. Other buildings alongside Furnival's Inn that were demolished included Ridler's Family Hotel, which had

8 *Furnival's Inn,*
the second building, drawn
by T H Shepherd in 1828.

FURNIVALS INN

been the site of a hostelry since the 14th century when it was known as The Crowne, and one of Carlo Gatti's cafés. The **present front of the Prudential Building** dates from 1899–1906. This remains one of London's Victorian Gothic showpieces, an overwhelming mass of flaming red brick and terracotta with tall ranges all amply gabled, and a huge central tower crowned by a pyramidal roof with a spike.

We now turn left under the tower and a tall rib-vaulted archway into the heart of the complex. Passing on the right Chancery Hall (occasionally open for exhibitions), built about 1900 and lavishly glazed inside in yellow tiles, continue through into the first small courtyard and note on the right-hand side a plum-coloured plaque to Charles Dickens.

Dickens lived at No.15 Furnival's Inn in 1834–7, first as a bachelor and then in the early days of his marriage. Here he began *Pickwick Papers* in 1836 before moving to larger premises in Doughty Street (now the Dickens House museum). Dickens knew the whole area to the north of Furnival's Inn well and set many of the scenes in his novels here: Bleeding Heart Yard (p 43) features in *Little Dorrit*, and Hatton Garden and Saffron Hill (p 41) in *Oliver Twist*.

The court opens out, under a very wide and dramatic arched bridge with Tudor-style windows, into the generous main court, now called **Waterhouse Square**. The surrounding terracotta buildings are

a delight. Straight ahead is a little alcove with a bronze bust of Charles Dickens and a tablet recording his work on *Pickwick Papers*. Another tablet notes the work of EPR Architects and Ove Arup engineers in 1993, when new work added a deep back range with sleek purple granite cladding extending north over what was once a part of Greville Street (pp 43,61), connecting Brooke Street and Leather Lane.

In the centre of the paved courtyard is a glass dome surrounded by seating. If you peer into the dome which lights offices below, you see suspended a bright green Calder-like mobile. To your left is a bronze sculpture of two winged angels gathering up a dead soldier, by F V Blundestone (1922), commemorating the men of the Prudential who died in WW I.

Walk through the passage past the sign 'No.1' and emerge in the pedestrianised part of **LEATHER LANE**, where we are going to turn right. If you are there during the week there are likely to be street traders in the non-pedestrianised portion of the street just out of sight to your left: Leather Lane boasts one of the oldest street markets in London. There has been much speculation about the origin of the name. It was almost certainly not from the leather traders who later carried on business here. It may come from leveroun, the old French word for greyhound, or from the personal name Leofrun. The most likely derivation is from Soke Lane, the lane leading to the Soke of

Portpoole (p 11), which in contemporary Flemish was rendered as Le Vrunelane. By 1240, Samson Enganet from Flanders owned part of this soke, and the small farm track was formed and named at this time. The transformation was as follows: Le Vrune–Lyverune–Lyver–Lither–Leather Lane by the 17th century.

By the end of Elizabeth I's reign Stow called it "a turning to the fields, lately replenished with houses". The street market, established when the street developed into a down-at-heel district during the 17th century, is depicted on Ogilby's map of 1677. In 1720 Strype notes several inns 'all indifferent', but says the east side was by then all brick-built. Behind these houses were several yards for stables and coach houses for the wealthy inhabitants of Hatton Garden nearby.

By the 19th century Leather Lane (Fig 9) was described as a very poor neighbourhood with thieves, beggars and Italian organ grinders, but there was a flourishing working-class market on Friday and Saturday nights, after weekly wages had been paid. In the 1930s the market was quieter, selling fruit and vegetables. In the 1950s and 1960s the influx of office workers into Holborn made it one of London's busiest lunchtime markets. It now sells food, clothes and general goods, mainly to nearby office workers, with 150 licensed stalls.

Turn right and walk towards the main

road. To our left, under a concrete arcade, is the **Sir Christopher Hatton**, named after the Elizabethan courtier of whom we shall hear more (p 35). He is depicted on a free-standing pub sign wearing a very large emerald ring. The large modern block here covers the site of two once famous old inns which stood side by side. The Old Bell, first mentioned in 1538, had a galleried structure dating from the 17th century (Fig 10). It was the last galleried inn north of the Thames when it was demolished in 1897, and the terminus of the last regular omnibus service from an inn between here and Uxbridge, Amersham and Wendover. The Black Bull next door was demolished in 1901, its courtyard being converted into dwellings. Dickens mentioned it as the place where Mr Lewsome in *Martin Chuzzlewit* took ill and was nursed by Mrs Gamp and Betsey Prig 'turn and turn about'.

The inns made way for the extension of the famous store Gamage's. Albert Walter Gamage, a farmer's son working as an assistant in a drapery shop in the City in 1878, took a watch to be repaired at Lindsey and Co. at No.127 Holborn. The watchmaker mentioned the need for a good hosiery shop in the area and that the shop next door was empty. With the help of a friend, Frank Arthur Spain, whom he bought out in 1881, Gamage rented the

9 Leather Lane looking south towards the main road (partly demolished 1898).

small shop with a 5-foot frontage at
No.128 on the corner with Leather Lane.
His motto over the door was *Tall Oaks
from Little Acorns Grow*. His policy was to
sell items cheaper than anyone else did. At
times manufacturers refused to supply him,
and he then bought large quantities from
small manufacturers, who made products
exclusively for the store.

Through the years Gamage added the
small old properties around the original
building. This resulted in a series of rooms,
passages, steps and ramps which made the
search for departments an adventure. By
the 1900s Gamage's stretched all the way
from Leather Lane to Hatton Garden.

Gamage's specialised in mail order
and was known as 'The People's Popular
Emporium'. The shop outfitted the Boy
Scouts. One could buy explorers' tables,
mosquito nets, collapsible urinals and
much more. Departments included a zoo,
a toy department (with a large model
railway) and a motoring department. Here
Gamage was said to have lain in state at
his death in 1930, guarded by salesmen.
The store closed in 1972, moving to
Bowmans in Camden Town and Oxford
Street, but closed for good in 1975.

The huge, unlovely building now on
the site is **No.120 Holborn**, by Richard
Seifert & Partners 1974–81. The whole

*10 The inn yard of the Old Bell Inn
(demolished 1897).*

development covers 2.25 acres; the freehold changed hands in August 1997 for £97 million. The block, with its plum-tinted glazing between pale stone bands, was described by Charles McKean in *The Times* in 1980 as a "lumpen, heavy-handed mass of tinted reflective glass and granite...the building is monstrous: a monstrously wasted opportunity" given its important site on Holborn Circus.

HOLBORN CIRCUS is at the north-western end of a major piece of Victorian street improvement, the Holborn Viaduct scheme (1863–9). Previously, all traffic had had to dip down to the valley of the Fleet running along present-day Farringdon Road, and climb again into Newgate and the City. The whole development cost over £2 million, including the making of Charterhouse Street (to our left, p 40).

Of the 19th-century buildings in Holborn Circus only **No.1–3 Hatton Garden**, dated 1870, remains. It is now the National Westminster Bank and is of yellow brick with windows in stone panels, surmounted by a balustrade. Opposite is a triangular patch of green with a fine view of the square stone tower of St Andrew's Holborn (Wren). As the church is not in Camden, we do not describe it here.

On the island in the centre, straddling the border between Camden and the City, is a bronze statue of Prince Albert on parade as a Field Marshal. Rather oddly for an officer, he is shown not saluting but raising his hat, in the direction of the City. The statue is the work of Charles Bacon, unveiled in January 1874. On either side of the oblong plinth are bronze plaques of Britannia and of Prince Albert, and reliefs commemorating the Great Exhibition and the third Royal Exchange; at either end are bronze figures of Commerce and Peace. The plinth was donated anonymously (originally) by a City businessman, Mr Charles Oppenheimer, who paid £2,000 for the central figure.

We are now on the corner of **HATTON GARDEN**. All of the district north of High Holborn bounded by Leather Lane to the west and Saffron Hill to the east was once known as Hatton Garden, but long before Christopher Hatton acquired the land in the 1570s this was the garden of the Bishops of Ely, remembered in Ely Place (p 37).

The medieval Bishops of Ely were so powerful in the Church and in the State that they needed a palace, chapel and grounds in London. At first they lodged at the Temple, but fell out with the Knights Templar. In 1272 John de Kirkeby, Henry III's Treasurer, acquired land in the then rural parish of St Andrew's. He was later made Bishop of Ely and built a great hall and chambers, which he bequeathed to the see as a London palace. By 1300 a chapel dedicated to St Etheldreda (p 38) had been built beside it, probably by Bishop William de Luda, bishop from 1290 to 1298. Building took about a century, resulting in a large courtyard with a hall facing it, a chapel built on a pre-existing undercroft left over from a much earlier building (which we cannot trace) and extensive 14-acre gardens. A 7-acre vineyard and an orchard were added in 1336. The palace stood on a hill and was visible for some distance around.

In 1328 the young Philippa of Hainault spent the night here before her wedding in York to the 15-year-old King Edward III. Their son John of Gaunt lived at the palace from 1381 until his death in 1399, after his former home (the Savoy Palace) had been wrecked by Wat Tyler's mob during the Peasants' Revolt. Here Shakespeare has Gaunt reflect, as he lies dying, on "This royal throne of kings, this sceptred isle. . . this blessed plot, this earth, this realm, this England" (*Richard II*, Act II). Shakespeare also noted the fine strawberries grown here, considered to be the finest in London, especially in Elizabethan times. He mentions them in *Richard III*, when Gloucester asks the Bishop of Ely to send for some. A popular Strawberrie Fayre is now held in Ely Place each year, as near as possible to 23 June, St Etheldreda's feast day.

The gardens north of the palace were enclosed by a thorn hedge in which were wooden gates fitted with locks and keys. The inner gardens were for the Bishop's use, and railings and locked doors separated the great garden and 'grassyard' from the vineyard. The meadow was mown

11 Sir Christopher Hatton at the height of his glory. What appears to be a large emerald ring on his right hand, doubtless copied as such in the crude modern inn-sign, is actually the pendant hanging from the chain about his neck.

every year and its grass and hay were sold; a tithe of the proceeds went to St Andrew's Church.

The Bishops of Ely used to rent out rooms to the nobility and court officials, since their household never occupied the whole palace. The Earl of Warwick (later Duke of Northumberland) lived here, and here the council met and planned the conspiracy that led to the execution of Protector Somerset (1552). Both he and Thomas Wriothesley, the last of Henry VIII's Chancellors, made unsuccessful attempts to gain part of the palace for themselves.

Christopher Hatton (1540–91, Fig 11) succeeded where the others had failed. He had first caught the young Queen Elizabeth I's eye at an entertainment given by students at the Inner Temple in 1561.

Sir Christopher Hatton he danced with grace, He'd a very fine form, and a very fine face.

He progressed to become the Queen's manager in the House of Commons by 1572 and was made Lord Chancellor, to the fury of more senior lawyers, in 1587. In 1576 Elizabeth obliged Bishop Cox, whom she detested, to let a 21-year lease on the gatehouse (on the site of the green space opposite us), most of the front courtyard and all 14 acres of gardens and orchard to her favourite Hatton for £10 a year, 10 loads of hay and one red rose picked at midsummer. The Bishop maintained his right to walk in the gardens and gather 20 bushels of roses annually.

Hatton undertook to repair the gatehouse and to make his portion of Ely Palace 'a convenient dwelling'. Taking full advantage of this phrase he built Hatton House, to the west and slightly north of the episcopal palace. The queen gave him the freehold for just under £1,900, the amount he had laid out in building. Like other favourites of Elizabeth, Hatton spent more than he could afford on houses he did not need in the hope of entertaining the Queen. He built the vast fabric of Holdenby in Northamptonshire, which he visited but rarely, and yet when the owner and builder of the neighbouring Kirby died he did not hesitate to buy and complete that house too.

It was from Hatton House that Hatton drove in 1587 to Westminster in great state for his installation as Lord Chancellor. The queen frequently visited him here. In 1590 she visited the house for a secret meeting with the French Ambassador, and on another occasion she went to inspect Hatton's contingent of 100 men-at-arms, which like many other citizens he had raised to resist the Armada. The queen also visited Hatton here in 1591 when he was on his deathbed, worn out by her demands to repay her his debts of £40,000.

The house passed to his nephew William Newport, who took Christopher Hatton's name. He married Lady Elizabeth Cecil, daughter of the 1st Earl of Exeter. She retained the house after Christopher

Hatton II's death 6 years later and her second marriage in 1598 to the lawyer Sir Edward Coke. They quarrelled constantly and disputed the marriage of their daughter. James I intervened, and the girl was married to Sir John Villiers, brother of the court favourite. A banquet for the King was held at the house (Lady Hatton refusing Coke entrance), which James greatly enjoyed: he knighted four of Lady Hatton's friends on the spot. After Coke had been dismissed from his post as Chief Justice in 1616 because of his opposition to the encroachments of royal prerogative his wife left him, living supreme at Hatton House until her death in 1646, by popular tradition carried off by the devil. Her Thursday 'At Homes' were great society occasions. She rebutted the attempts of four Bishops of Ely to dislodge her, even spending a brief period in the Fleet Prison for ignoring an injunction not to pull down buildings.

Christopher Hatton III, a Royalist in exile after the Civil war, was hard up and decided to lease the Hatton estate for building. He made over Hatton House to a Robert Smyth on a 200-year lease in 1654, but then leased it again in 1658 to a Robert Johnson, extending the lease for a further 1000 years. The development of the estate followed swiftly. On Newcourt's map of 1658 one can still see the walled garden with formal alleys and a central fountain stretching between Lither Lane and Saffron Hill to what is now Hatton Wall (p 46). The next year, in 1659, John

Evelyn noted in his diary that he had gone "to see the foundations now laying for a long streete, and buildings in Hatton Garden, designed for a little towne; lately an ample Garden". Such building outside the City was illegal, but in September 1661 Hatton obtained a pardon from Charles II, who made him Baron Hatton of Kirby and gave him a licence to continue building. Bishop Matthew Wren, newly released from imprisonment (see p 38), came home to find the former garden of Ely Palace laid out for building, and tried in vain to get an injunction against the builders. Baron Hatton's son, the 1st Viscount Hatton (d.1706), and the Bishops of Ely continued to dispute until 1697, when the bishop accepted £100 annual rent from Hatton as compensation for the land wrested from the bishops in the 1570s. By then Lord Hatton was getting considerably more than that in annual income from the buildings.

Abraham Arlidge, 'carpenter' (member, later Master of the Carpenters Company; we would call him a property developer) began a comprehensive scheme designed for merchants and others who wanted to move out of the City but not too far. The last of his 372 houses was completed in 1694, when he made a survey for Lord Hatton. The estate was planned on the lines of Covent Garden and Southampton (now Bloomsbury) Square, with uniform terraces flanking wide streets. It was very grand in the early 18th century.

Hawksmoor called Hatton Street "one of the best streets in London", and Strype noted in 1720 that it was well inhabited by gentry. Although never as expensive as Covent Garden, it was an oasis of wealth in the generally poor area north of Holborn. In 1696 it provided about a third of the total rates assessment for the parish of St Andrew's, Holborn.

Present-day Hatton Garden was known as Hatton Street until the mid-18th century. It was developed using standard plots with a 22-foot street frontage, for which a £6 12s ground rent was charged. Most of the plots were taken by speculators like Arlidge. Leases were generally 42 or 51 years, although Hatton was willing to negotiate up to 99 years. Hatton Street was for gentlemen, merchants and aristocracy. The earliest houses looked much like those in New Square, Lincoln's Inn (p 80): redbrick terraces, with panelled interiors, generally assessed at 10 hearths under the hearth tax introduced under Charles II.

In 1762 the 3rd and last Viscount Hatton died. His property passed to the Earl of Winchelsea, and subsequently to William, Earl of Mansfield – the famous Lord Chief Justice and owner of Kenwood – together with George Finch Hatton. In 1785 they sold off the Hatton Garden estate in lots by auction (320 dwelling houses, stables, outbuildings and nine Public Houses in Hatton Garden, Charles

Street, Great Kirby Street, Cross Street, Hatton Wall and Leather Lane).

Until the early 19th century no shops were permitted at this lower end of the street, and it was still an 'esteemed situation for gentry' in the 1820s. It is the only street in the area to feature in Boyle's *Court Guide* in 1829, when many surgeons and solicitors were living here.

Hatton Garden is now famous as the centre of the diamond trade. Some jewellers were working in gold and silver in the street by the late 1830s. Tallis's street directory has 12, although only one is identified in the street view as a shop. The trade in diamonds (especially in rough diamonds) expanded dramatically in the 1870s after the discovery of the Kimberley diamond fields in 1867. Many dealers in Hatton Garden moved from watch-making to become importers of precious stones, jewellers and diamond merchants. In 1870 there was only one diamond cutter in all London. During the 1870s Dutch cutters were lured to London, but proved expensive. English gem cutters were then recruited, under a policy supported by the Worshipful Company of Turners and Baroness Burdett-Coutts. Most firms were owned by Dutch or other foreign merchants, but with English workers.

The Diamond Syndicate of ten firms was set up in 1890, in agreement with De Beers, from whose mines and through whom most of the world's rough diamond production was and still is sold. The syndicate moved to Holborn Viaduct in the early 1890s, and later to Charterhouse Street. It developed into the Diamond Trading Co., formed in 1934, which sold diamonds, while the Diamond Corporation sorted them.

The Hatton Garden area retains an international reputation as London's jewellery quarter. There are many hundreds of local businesses and over 40 shops, which represent the largest jewellery retail cluster in the UK. This is a street where an oil sheikh can buy a diamond for over £50,000 or a young man or woman a ring for £50. It is said there is a wedding proposal every 15 minutes here, and the wedding business is worth over £1.4 billion per annum.

The west side of the street, where we are standing, has a wide pavement (in front of Seifert's development) with trees and benches, and a rather Parisian air. Diamond shops abound. If we cross the road the view to the left is of the bell tower of St Peter's Italian Church, in the heart of Little Italy (p 48). One of Italy's most famous sons lodged in Hatton Garden at No.5, which bears a dark bronze plaque with a bas-relief portrait and clasped hands. This is dedicated to Guiseppe Mazzini (1805–72), the Italian patriot who stayed here in 1841–2 (see also pp 48,56). Mazzini inspired Italy in its struggle for freedom. When he was in exile in London

he taught English nearby, above a barber's shop, and set up a school at No.5 Greville Street (p 61), supported by Carlyle and Rossetti. No.7 has an imposing, rather dirty, classical façade with impressive banded rustication.

Now look for a narrow alley through No.8 Hatton Garden, with a grimy metal grille above, and a gas lamp-post with a Mitre sign around it. This is **MITRE COURT** (shown on some maps as Ely Court), into which we now turn. It leads past a charming pub, the **Old Mitre**, built in the 18th century on the site of a tavern put up by Bishop Goodrich in 1546 for the use of the servants of Ely Palace. Note the stone mitre painted bright blue attached to the brickwork, which may have come from the bishops' gatehouse. Queen Elizabeth I is said to have danced the maypole around a cherry tree here; the preserved trunk inside the tavern is said to mark the dividing line between Hatton's and Ely's parts of the garden. In 1985 13th-century tiles from part of the medieval cloister of the Bishop of Ely's chapel were found near here, and it is thought that they continued under the back yard of the Mitre, and possibly into Mitre Court as well. We could well be walking over buried treasure.

Mitre Court leads into **ELY PLACE**, one of the last private roads in London, guarded by impressive iron gates and top-hatted frock-coated beadles. The licensing hours of the Mitre, and the time of closing of the gates of Ely Place, were until comparatively recently set by the justices of the peace of the Isle of Ely (see p 14).

After Hatton gained the freehold of the Bishop's estate the palace itself gradually fell into disrepair and disuse. In 1620 Gondomar, the Spanish ambassador, was living at Ely Palace, and there was much unrest at the thought that the chapel was being used by Spanish Jesuits. Gondomar was very unpopular with Londoners, who held him responsible for the execution of Sir Walter Raleigh. An attempt was made on his life, and the redoubtable Lady Hatton refused him the use of the garden as a short cut. In 1622 the palace was granted to the Duke of Lennox and Richmond; he died in 1624 and his widow remained in possession until Bishop Matthew Wren, uncle of Christopher, secured possession shortly before he was imprisoned as a suspected Catholic sympathiser in 1640. In 1642 Ely Palace itself was used as a prison for Royalists and then as a hospital for wounded Parliamentarian soldiers. It was so dilapidated by 1659 that portions of it were demolished.

At the Restoration in 1660 Bishop Wren regained possession, and Ely Palace continued to be the London residence of Bishops of Ely until the 18th century, although it was allowed to decay. Some of the buildings were let out as lodgings. The poet William Cowper (1731–1800) studied law here with a solicitor, which depressed him so much that he quitted London on the verge of madness. In the 1760s the Government considered Ely Palace as a possible site for a new Fleet Prison, but the gentry in Hatton Garden successfully petitioned against the Bill. In 1772 the Bishop of Ely transferred to the Crown all his rights here in return for £6500 and an annuity of £200, and moved to Ely House in Dover Street, Mayfair. Charles Cole, architect and surveyor, bought the site for £7600 and demolished all the buildings of Ely Palace apart from the chapel.

Brick terraced houses were built on the site from 1773, and many of them survive. On the east side, opposite, most of the façades of First Rate 18th-century houses can still be seen: four storeys, three windows across, and wooden pedimented door surrounds, all painted white. Staying on the west side, turn left past another original house at No.13, housing St Etheldreda's Convent, towards the end of the road, which is formed by a brick wall with three rounded arches bearing terracotta tablets dated 1881. Ely Place was from its inception a cul-de-sac, because it abutted the Hatton Estate. At the end on this side of the street looms the grandiose, French-Renaissance-style, early-20th-century **Audrey House** (Nos.15–20), which when first built in 1904 housed many diamond merchants. But tucked in beside it we come upon the church of

St Etheldreda's. This is the old chapel of the Bishop of Ely's Palace, a miraculous survival with a magnificent west window.

St Etheldreda's was built in the 1290s as a private chapel by Bishop William de Luda on the site of an earlier structure. Its arrangement in two storeys is typical of private chapels, for example Paris's Sainte Chapelle. The crypt or undercroft of an earlier date, with 8-foot thick walls, incorporates still older walls which may have been part of a Roman basilica. In the 19th century excavations revealed Roman foundations dating back to the 3rd century, and there may have been a Romano-British church here. Roman glass bottles were found, as well as Roman nails and a marble bowl of Roman or Ancient British origin.

St Etheldreda (630–679) was a Saxon Abbess of Ely, daughter of Anna, King of the East Angles. Part of her hand is kept in the church. She is sometimes known as St Audry, hence *Audrey House* next door. At the fair of St Audry in Ely cheap necklaces made of worthless glass beads used to be sold under the name *tawdry laces*, which gives us the adjective *tawdry*.

In 1772, when the Bishops of Ely moved to Dover Street, the church became a proprietary chapel (one in which the minister is supported wholly by his congregation's contributions). In 1836 it was sold to the Welsh Episcopalians. In 1873 the whole of Ely Place was put up for sale and bought for £5400 by a Roman

Catholic organisation (the Rosminian Fathers), which effected many restorations, having found the chapel in a state of "inconceivable filth". Catholic mass was said there in 1874 for the first time in 250 years. St Etheldreda's is one of the very few English medieval churches in the possession of Roman Catholics, and was the first in England to be returned to them.

It was scheduled an ancient monument in 1925. In WW II its Victorian glass and the chestnut roof were badly damaged, but the West Window of 1300 mercifully survived. Its Early Decorated window tracery has been judged some of the finest in existence. The stained glass is modern.

A visit inside is a must. The corridor leading into the chapel was once part of the open cloister added in about 1373 by Bishop Arundel; it is where Henry VIII is said to have first met Cranmer. Within is a barrel-vaulted upper church of five bays with dramatic stained glass and statues of 16th-century martyrs of the Catholic Church, placed here during the restoration completed in the early 1960s. The crypt below has more colourful stained glass, and a model of Ely Palace in the 16th century. Not accessible to the casual visitor is a sculptured Holy Family over the rear door (Fig 12).

On leaving the church, turn right towards the gatehouse. At No.39 (demolished) Sir Charles Barry (1795–1860), later architect of the Houses of Parliament, lived as a young man from 1820 to 1827.

Under the Bishops this part of their palace enjoyed rights of sanctuary. By the 1680s, the "Liberty of Saffron Hill, Hatton Garden and Ely Rents in the Parish of St Andrew Holborn" had its own extra-parochial administration (see pp 13–14); when Ely Place was built in 1773 its name was added to the title of the Liberty. However, being Crown property Ely Place was in 1842 made a separate entity under the Ely Place Improvements Act, which provided for elected commissioners responsible for paving, lighting, cleaning

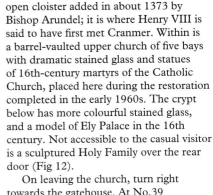

12 Sculpture over the rear door of St Etheldreda's.

and improving the street. The commissioners were also empowered to appoint their own constables to patrol their little empire, and this meant that metropolitan police were not allowed to enter the street except by invitation. Those who contravened the provisions of the Act could, however, be hauled before the local justices by the Ely Place constables, so the former rights of 'sanctuary' had by then been completely suppressed. In 1899, most of the commissioners' powers were transferred to the metropolitan borough of Holborn, but the Place is still administered by Commissioners under the 1842 Act. The six Commissioners are elected by the ratepayers, who are mainly solicitors, with a few diamond merchants. At the time of writing they include Father Kit Cunningham of St Etheldreda's and W Carling, father of the former captain of the England Rugby team. The beadles maintain order, for example ensuring that bicycles are not chained to railings, and that no skips or containers are delivered. However, the watchman no longer calls the hours, as he did until 1939. An attempt was made after WW II to revive this custom, but there were complaints after the first night and it was stopped.

Pass through the gates, and either return to our starting point (Chancery Lane Tube station) and your transport home, or proceed to Route 3.

Route 3
By the valley of the River Fleet

A walk circling the former slums of the Fleet valley and ending at Farringdon station; or continuing into Little Italy by Route 4.

From Holborn Circus (p 34), approached if you will along Holborn from the Chancery Lane Tube station, take **CHARTERHOUSE STREET**, a long, straight street made in 1869–75 between Holborn Circus and Smithfield Meat Market, whose green domes you can see ahead across the valley of the Fleet river. The street, formerly entirely within the City, has since 1994 marked the boundary with Camden (and, beyond Farringdon Road, the boundary between the City and Islington). **No.1** is a 1950s neo-Georgian building with a curved front, which attempts to harmonise with the houses of Ely Place (p 37). The next building, **Nos.11–15**, the HQ of the Diamond Trading Company, by Chapman Taylor 1976–9, is very different in style. Its restless front with projecting flat green-glazed bays of different heights has two floors clad in Portland roach (pitted Portland stone) with inset slit windows. Above are brown metal panels with

windows, some jettied out. A covered bridge crosses to the office building opposite, **No.2**, which since 1957 has housed the offices of the sorting staff employed by the Diamond Corporation.

By the steps at the side of the building, which lead down into Saffron Hill, pause and reflect on the changes brought about by street improvements in Victorian times. The mid-19th-century development of Holborn Circus, Charterhouse Street, Holborn Viaduct and Farringdon Road required the wholesale demolition of a notorious slum district that had formed along the Fleet Valley. In 1720 Strype described Saffron Hill as "pestered with small and ordinary alleys and courts taken up by the meaner sort of people, especially the east side unto the Town Ditch". He noted that many of these small alleys led to small boarded bridges over the polluted river. Flimsy wooden buildings were run up by speculators and landlords in courtyards and every waste space, with the flanking houses continually in danger of collapse. Although from 1737 night watchmen were on patrol, their small numbers coupled with the large number of alehouses open all night seem to have rendered these arrangements for maintaining law and order ineffective.

Barbarous conditions of life and high levels of crime throughout the 18th century and into the 19th century brought notoriety to the area. The Poor Law

Commission's report of 1839 called it a filthy district, and it was immortalised in *Oliver Twist* as the haunt of Fagin. The rookeries here were as bad as any in London, and overcrowding and death rates worsened in the 19th century.

Some 4000 people were displaced as the City authorities, intent on "shovelling out the poor" between the 1830s and 1870s, created what was long known as 'Farringdon Waste'. The name is derived from the ancient City ward known as Farringdon Without (p 10); Alderman Farindon, a goldsmith, and his son controlled the ward for over 80 years from 1281. Farringdon Road, which crosses Charterhouse Street at the traffic lights ahead, was projected as early as 1838 and legislated for in 1840, but not begun until the mid-1840s. Under the name Victoria Street it opened in 1856. The intention was to improve health, morals and traffic circulation by covering over the malarial Fleet, clearing slums and driving a thoroughfare through narrow streets which had been "almost impassable for carriages". Work started at Holborn Hill and moved northwards. The new developments almost obliterated the infamous Chick Lane (previously Chicken Lane), which was also known as West Street; it led to Smithfield market. In West Street, near where we are now, stood a Red Lion tavern on the corner of Brewhouse Yard, which for the last 100 years of its life

was a common lodging house and the resort of thieves, a hiding place with trap doors, sliding panels and escape hatches onto the Fleet. The highwayman Jack Sheppard often hid here. It was pulled down in 1844.

Although Victoria Street (unfortunately synonymous with several other Victoria Streets in London) was opened in 1856, it took another 20 years for the new street to be built up, largely with warehouses. The Metropolitan Railway terminus appeared in 1863, and Victoria Street was renamed Farringdon Road (p 47). The area was still open enough in 1878 to accommodate the stones of Temple Bar for some 10 years before they were removed to Theobalds Park in Hertfordshire.

Walk down the steps beside the Diamond Trading Company building. This is now private land, but pedestrian access is usually no problem. At the foot of the steps, note through the gates on the left a series of steps leading up through flower beds and shrubs, almost like hanging gardens, to **VIADUCT BUILDINGS**. This is on the site of Union Court, which was demolished when Charterhouse Street was formed. The four-storey 1874 building at the top originally contained working-class flats designed by Sir Horace Jones for the City. The brick-built centre and ends project forward, and the intervening delicate elliptical iron arcades, with pierced balustrades, are painted white. These are

now offices called **St Andrew House**.

Continue up the narrow street, between tall buildings. We are now in **SAFFRON HILL**. The gardens of the Bishop of Ely were famous for fruit (p 34), but they were also famous for saffron, which was grown here soon after its introduction into Cambridgeshire in the 14th century. Saffron was vital to disguise the taste of city dwellers' rancid meat. It was also thought to 'quiet the brain and strengthen the heart'. Eventually, it gave its name to the hilly road running through the Bishop's estate. This was first known as Gold Lane, which John Stow as early as 1598 described as "sometime a filthy passage into the fields, now both sides built with small tenements". The noisome vapours from the Fleet nearby promoted squalor and poverty and bred disease: this area suffered particularly seriously during the plague outbreak in 1665.

This end of Saffron Hill was the narrow Field Lane, most of which disappeared during the Holborn Valley improvements of the 1860s. In 1720 Strype called it "narrow and mean, full of Butchers and Tripe dressers because the Ditch runs at the back of their slaughterhouses, and carries away the filth". Dickens called Field Lane 'the emporium of petty larceny' and sketching it in *Oliver Twist* in 1837 wrote "stores of old iron and bones, and heaps of mildewy fragments of woollen stuff and linen, rust and rot in the grimy cellars".

Field Lane and Saffron Hill attracted much attention from Victorian social reformers such as Lord Shaftesbury, who said in the Lords on 28 February 1861 that he had found 314 rooms in 62 houses in 8 small courts off Holborn Hill with an average size of 8 feet by less than 4 feet, in which 179 people were living. "It is impossible to imagine the physical and moral evil which resulted from these circumstances and to describe the fearful effects on the population." A Sabbath school, started in a back room in Caroline Yard in November 1841, became the Field Lane Ragged School, and after it moved to 65 West Street (Chick Lane) in 1842, part of the premises also became a Night Refuge. In 1857 a separate night refuge for destitute women and girls was opened in Hatton Yard (Fig 13). *The Times* wrote an article about the Refuge on Christmas Eve 1858 which led to many visitors and thousands of letters and gifts. During the harsh winter of 1860–61 the newspapers gave much publicity to generous donations to the refuge.

The building of Charterhouse Street forced the Field Lane Refuge to move, at first to Hatton Wall, but street improvements (this time the building of Clerkenwell Road) again forced a move in 1877, to Vine Hill (p 55).

Saffron Hill, as a poor area, attracted poor immigrants. The Irish arrived in large numbers during the 1840s, and a Roman Catholic mission was soon opened. At **No.141–2**, where Viaduct Buildings rejoins the street, a Chapel of the Holy

Family was opened in 1854. Father Kyne started a scheme for the building of a cathedral in the street, but failed to raise sufficient cash.

The Apostolic Exarchate for Ukrainians

13   Field Lane women's night refuge.

bought the church in the late 1940s and used it until 1967; a few years later it was demolished.

We now reach **GREVILLE STREET**, where we turn left. At the far end of the street rises the development, clad in pink granite, around Waterhouse Square (p 31). This has covered the original Greville Street, named after Fulke Greville (p 28), whose grounds extended over the site. The street here as far as Leather Lane was until July 1937 known as Charles Street, probably named after Charles II, during whose reign it was first developed. The new Hatton Garden Estate was cut off as far as possible from Saffron Hill, already ramshackle, and only a small paved alley led from Charles Street into Saffron Hill at this point. Strype in 1720 said it was "very ill, and called by some, Pissing Alley".

As we walk up Greville Street (see also p 61) we can see that, as in Hatton Garden, there are many manufacturing jewellers and diamond merchants, jewellery polishers and setters.

We now turn left again into cobbled **BLEEDING HEART YARD**, with late-19th-century warehouses. This was first built in the early 1680s by Arlidge (p 36) near the Bishop of Ely's back gate. He leased the old dungheap of Ely Palace, which had been used as a sty by swine in Field Lane and Saffron Hill. Stables were built around the yard, and blocked the bishop's northern entrance. Known locally

as "Alldridges Yard" it was never salubrious. In the 19th century the Yard was described in Dickens' *Little Dorrit*: Dorrit's prison friend Plornish the plasterer lived here.

One of the *Ingoldsby Legends* has Lady Elizabeth Hatton dancing one night in 1646 with a mysterious stranger, said to be the Devil. Lying on the cobbles next morning was her body, torn limb from limb, and her still bleeding, throbbing heart. However, the true origin of the name of the yard is somewhat less romantic. It derives from an old inn sign depicting a broken-hearted Virgin Mary. The sign was said to date from before the Reformation and hung from the pub, **The Bleeding Heart**, at the entrance to the yard. The pub declares it was established in 1746, although it has only recently opened as such. There are also signs (including one saying "Bleeding Hard to Find, but Worth it") to a fashionable bistro and restaurant in the corner of the yard. It has French chefs and offers over 400 different wines.

Return to Greville Street and turn right down the hill towards the Fleet valley. The most striking feature of the streetscape here is the fine Victorian gothic building on the right, whose main frontage we reach on p 47. But now we turn left to continue up Saffron Hill. A few doors further on the left is the **One Tun**, established in 1759. It claims to be one of only two pubs left with

this name, which means the largest barrel of beer: 4 hogsheads or 252 pints. Dickens mentions the pub in *Oliver Twist*, although the present building dates from 1875. Note in the centre of the façade a carved and painted barrel, nestling among barley and hops. Further along the street on the opposite side is a fine brick-built late-19th-century four-storey warehouse, of nine bays with windows recessed between shallow arches. At each end bay above the entrances are identical panels depicting a sailing ship in full sail, the date 1726 and a swan with the name L & Co. The warehouse was until WW II a ship binding works, where parts for ships were made.

At the crossroads with **ST CROSS STREET** (until 1937 known as Cross Street), turn right. The derelict land on our right was part of the site of Charles Barry's church, St Peter's the Apostle Saffron Hill, started in 1830 and opened in 1832 despite opposition from St Andrew Holborn. The district was separated from the parish in 1832 and became an independent parish in 1839. The church was designed in what Pevsner in 1952 called 'a meagre Tudor Gothic style' (Fig 14). It had space for 994 adults, with 789 free sittings to accommodate the poor of the area. It was not rebuilt after being partially destroyed in WW II, and its parish was combined with that of St Alban the Martyr (p 62). Offices were built on the corner with Saffron Hill in 1959. Opposite,

there is an ugly NCP car park, shoddily finished with red metal bands. This was the site of a Board school which was also bombed during WW II.

Turn back up St Cross Street and cross Saffron Hill. William Whiston (1667–1752), clergyman, mathematician and friend of Sir Isaac Newton, lived in Cross Street. **KIRBY STREET** joins from the left. It was developed at the same time as the rest of the Hatton Garden Estate from 1659, although that could not be guessed from the dull 20th-century office buildings now lining it. John Longland, the carpenter who worked on Wren's churches, had a hand in its development. The street was named after Lord Hatton's manor in Northamptonshire (p 35). At No.30 in 1796 William Godwin was introduced to his wife-to-be, Mary Wollstonecraft. When in 1814 their daughter Mary, the future Mrs Shelley, eloped with the poet to the Continent, it was coincidentally in Hatton Garden that the getaway carriage awaited her breathless arrival at 4 am.

Beyond Kirby Street, note **Nos.9 & 10 St Cross Street**, 18th-century houses which present gable ends to the street; No.10 has a small porch with scrolled

14 St Peter's the Apostle Saffron Hill, with what appears to be an old-clothes shop, H Myers at No.107, in the foreground. Drawing by R W Billings, 1839.

44

brackets and railings. Opposite these used
to be a large house with a chapel attached.
In the late 18th century it was used by
Swedenborg's disciples, and known as the
New Jerusalem Chapel. It was later used
by Scottish Presbyterians, who appointed
Edward Irving in 1822 (an interior highly
suitable to charismatic preachers is shown
in Fig 15). The 'Caledonian Church'
became very fashionable and attracted
crowds and carriages from the West End.
Irving later founded his own charismatic
sect, the Irvingites.

Backtrack slightly and turn into
HATTON PLACE, away from Kirby
Street. This was originally known as Hat
and Tun Yard, from the inn at its far end.
It opens up into a small car park, with to
our left **Chapel House**, recalling the site
of the chapel just mentioned. Here we can
see the backs of buildings in Hatton
Garden. Especially noticeable is the fire
escape behind the tall inter-war block
which is on the site of an old police station

*15 "A view of the painted recess, executed by
W Bradley Esq, in the New Jerusalem Church,
Cross Street, Hatton Garden, London". Drawn,
painted and etched by John Harwood and
published in 1830. The inscription in the semi-
dome reads "I am the First and the Last: I am
He that liveth and was dead, Behold I am He
that liveth for ever and ever. Look unto Me,
and be saved, all ye ends of the Earth, for I am
GOD and there is none else."*

mentioned in *Oliver Twist* (see also p 57). The small buildings to the right were gutted by incendiary bombs in 1941 but were rebuilt behind the façades, some being turned into small offices. Note the two elephant heads, a larger one to the left on **Tusker House** and a smaller one on **Little Tusker House** to the right: offices of a design company. At **No.11** (the last house on the right) barrel organs were made in the early 1890s by Alexander Capra and Co.

Passing under the arch of the **Hat and Tun** (the name is of course a pun on *Hatton*), whose Victorian exuberance is worth a glance, we emerge in **HATTON WALL**. As its name suggests, it replaced the high, thatched boundary wall of Hatton's estate. The street was developed in the 1670s.

Glance to the left at **No.59**, the London Jewellery Exchange, opened in 1982. At the time this was a new idea for Britain, imported from America. Here, diamond and jewellery dealers could buy and sell from each other as well as to the general public. It is still an exchange, but now only for the trade. Turn right past the Hat and Tun pub, and reach Saffron Hill again. East of Saffron Hill the street was until 1864 known as Vine Street, leading steeply down to the Ditch and a bridge across to Clerkenwell. This part disappeared in the making of Clerkenwell Road in the 1870s. Here the Field Lane Refuge was sited from

1871 to 1877. If we look back along Saffron Hill we can see on the left side a tall 1930s *moderne* white plaster building. Built as Onslow House, it was hailed as a masterpiece of industrial *art deco*, and housed the manufacture of 'Veritas' lamps and gas and electrical fittings by the firm of Falk, Stadelmann & Co. Swept by fire in the blitz of 1941, it was hit again in a V1 raid 3 years later and partly demolished. The building has been extended and refurbished as up-market apartments. A large blue post attached to its front surmounted by a flagpole bears the sign '**Ziggurat**', which is brought to mind by its stepped roof.

We have now reached the end of Saffron Hill. Here we meet the gentle incline of **CLERKENWELL ROAD**, a new thoroughfare laid out by the Metropolitan Board of Works in 1878 between Gray's Inn Road and Goswell Road and designed as a direct route from Shoreditch and the London Docks to Oxford Street. It cost £1.6 million, slicing through a maze of slums, and quickly became a tram route lined with warehouses. Provision was made for rehousing 1160 people. The road bears the name of the parish to the east, beyond the Farringdon Road under which the river Fleet now runs. The ancient Clerk's Well, which was sunk in the eastern bank of the river, was used by the medieval brothers of St John, and here parish clerks performed their miracle plays.

Turn left for a few yards to the corner of Hatton Garden, noting across the road the striking façade of the Italian church of St Peter's, described in detail in Route 4, *which you may choose to follow from here. But to continue this walk, finishing at Farringdon station,* retrace your steps down Clerkenwell Road, noting as you do so the fine view towards Clerkenwell Green, with the upper storey and open-work spire of St James' visible as well as the back of the neo-Palladian former Middlesex Sessions House, with a prominent lead-covered dome.

Cross Saffron Hill and pause where a short flight of steps leads off to the right. Hard by these steps, on the east side, is the sometime distribution depot of publishers John Murray. The next building to the east is the former Veritas House, once the headquarters of Falk, Stadelmann & Co. (see above). Turn, however, down the steps into **ONSLOW STREET**, named not after the well-known earl, but probably after one Richard Onslow, a Hatton Garden resident in 1677. On the west side once stood an Anglican Sunday school belonging to St Peter's, Saffron Hill and charmingly named the Children's Fresh Air Mission. Overlooking the far end of the street on the right is the back of the Ziggurat flats, former Onslow House.

Onslow Street ends in short **SAFFRON STREET**, into which we turn left. Saffron Street was known until 1936 as Castle

Street, after a tavern which had existed in nearby Saffron Hill since at least 1672. Castle Street was the birthplace in 1839 of the local antiquarian and topographical artist John Philipps Emslie (see also p 72). Very soon we reach **FARRINGDON ROAD** (see also p 41).

To your left is a 1960s post-office block, under refurbishment as flats at the time of writing and to be known as the Montgomery Building. Farringdon Road was long the venue for a famous second-hand book market which stretched from Clerkenwell to Charterhouse Street, along the Islington side of the street. It survived, much reduced, into the 1980s. The whole of that side is here taken up with a piece of Toytown architecture housing offices. Turn right along the Camden side, passing the Victorian **Nos.77–79** which unexpectedly house some offices of *The Guardian* and *The Observer* newspapers.

Continue south, keeping on the west, Camden, side of Farringdon Road. Marc Griffith's recently opened bespoke tailor's at **No.67** exemplifies how upmarket the district is becoming, as local properties are converted to luxury 'lofts'. **No.63** (Telescope House) has an old sign "Broadhurst, Clarkson & Co". It sells telescopes; such instruments have been manufactured on this site since 1830. **No.61** next door has a white plaque just above the pavement recording that these premises were totally destroyed by a Zeppelin raid on 8 September 1915 and were rebuilt in 1917. Just before No.57 we pass an archway labelled *1887: The Drill Hall*, which leads to a small yard and hall bearing the City of London arms. This was the base of the 2nd City of London Volunteers.

On the corner with Greville Street we reach the **Sir John Oldcastle** pub. This is worth a visit, if only for the historical vignettes of the area lining its walls. Oldcastle (c.1378–1417) lived further up Farringdon Road, near Mount Pleasant. A leader of the Lollards who had Wycliffe's works transcribed and distributed, he had a distinguished army career, but after the accession of Henry V he was examined and condemned as a heretic; after escape and recapture he was simultaneously hanged and burned to death. Shakespeare portrayed him as Prince Hal's boon companion, originally naming the character Oldcastle, but changing the name to Falstaff when descendants complained that he should not be so ridiculed. Sir John Fastolf (1378–1459), often alleged to be the inspiration for Shakespeare's character, was also an army commander in France, but there the connection ends.

Across Greville Street is the dramatic polychromatic building we encountered earlier. Boasting a corner turret with conical roof, and a row of cast-iron lancet windows with tracery, this veritable 'Venetian Palace' of 1873 by Harding & Bond, originally built for the engravers Bradbury, Wilkinson & Co., has recently been renovated and turned into apartments.

Across Farringdon Road, and thus in the borough of Islington, Farringdon station, where this walk ends, was long the Metropolitan Railway's railhead for the Holborn area. For 14 years, from 1922, it bore the name 'Farringdon & High Holborn', which optimistic title is still inscribed on the façade, though the entrance is now in the significantly named Cowcross Street (cattle were once driven this way to Smithfield market).

From here you can take an Underground or mainline train to your destination, or walk the short remaining stretch of Farringdon Road to Charterhouse Street and back up the hill to Holborn Circus.

Around Little Italy

Walk best undertaken at the weekend, if you wish to see inside St Peter's Italian Church, which is open only at weekends, and then erratically. Buses on route 55 from Oxford Circus, stop right outside it. Alternatively, you can reach the starting point in 5–10 minutes by walking from Farringdon station.

Beginning on the north side of Clerkenwell Road (p 46), near its junction with Back Hill, this walk takes us through 'Little Italy', an area where Italian migrants congregated in the 19th century, and which retains a strong Italian accent to this day. Political upheavals after the Napoleonic wars led many exiles to seek refuge in London, men such as Gabriele Rossetti, father of the Pre-Raphaelite painter, and Mazzini (p 37). Political refugees were followed by craftsmen and itinerant musicians, at first mainly from northern or central Italy. Italian immigration rose steadily from 1851 to 1891 from just over 1500 to over 5000 and rapidly thereafter, doubling by 1901, the immigrants by then mainly from the south. Within London, most Italians settled in the Holborn area: its attractions to craftsmen were its central location between the City and the West End, and its existing manufacturing base. Rents were fairly low because the houses were in a poor state.

The first Italian migrants often lived in better houses in Charles Street (Greville Street) and Hatton Garden, but as street musicians and plaster-figure makers arrived they settled in poorer housing in Leather Lane and Saffron Hill. Later immigrants tended to congregate in Back Hill and its neighbouring streets, where one in ten of the entire London Italian population once lived. The district was very overcrowded. Surveys in the 1880s found that conditions in Italian households were the worst of any group; in Little Italy there was usually more than one family per room.

The poorer Italian immigrants were often given accommodation by a *padrone*, who brought them over and found them employment in return for some or all of their wages. This system was well established by the 1840s. Most Italian migrants took to the streets as barrel-organ grinders, street musicians, figure sellers, knife grinders or ice-cream vendors. (Italians are credited with introducing ice cream and water ices, or hokey pokey, to London.) In winter they sold hot chestnuts or potatoes, or did asphalting. Others, skilled craftsmen, set up in business as mosaic or terrazzo artists, or as makers of cutlery, picture-frames, looking-glasses, barometers, or instruments musical and scientific.

The Italian community which started here in the early 19th century as one of single, transient males gradually became more settled as women were invited over and children were born here. Italian clubs and institutions sprang up: the Italian Benevolent Society, founded in 1861, which campaigned against the abuse of children; then the church and school, and an Italian working men's club (p 56); and in 1884 the Italian Hospital in Queen Square, some way to the west. Migration away from Little Italy occurred at the end of the 19th century, and again in the 1960s, but the area is still a focus of Italian spiritual and social life.

Our appropriate first port of call is **St Peter's Italian Church**. The church's construction followed a Europe-wide fund-raising campaign to give London's Italians their own church. It might have been known as the 'Church of All Nations', but was dedicated by Cardinal Wiseman on 16 April 1863 as the 'Chiesa Italiana di San Pietro'. Designed by the Irish architect John Miller Bryson, it has a tall, narrow two-bay front squeezed between houses, with a very Italianate double-arched loggia. Enter, if you can, to view its large interior (Fig 16), which takes the form of an Early Christian basilica, and is an exact replica of San Cristogno in Trastevere in Rome. The walls and ceiling were painted by Piedmontese artists in the 1880s. Singers

Caruso and Gigli both performed here. Outside, in the porch, is a plaque by Mancini representing a lifeboat, and recalling the tragic sinking in 1940 of the liner *Arandora Star* while carrying Italian internees to Canada. Although now the main entrance to the church, the porch was once a side entrance, facing onto an erstwhile George Yard. This, along with an Italian school which occupied it (though earlier founded in Hatton Garden), was obliterated in the 1878 construction (p 46) of Clerkenwell Road, which also sliced through Saffron Hill.

On the Sunday nearest to 16 July the traffic is banished from Clerkenwell Road and the pavements are lined by spectators of the annual Procession of Our Lady of Carmel. Starting from the Back Hill side of St Peter's (p 52), colourful floats make stately progress along this stretch of Clerkenwell Road, then south along Farringdon Road, returning to the church via St Cross Street and Leather Lane. The event dates from 1883, when it was the first Roman Catholic procession in London since the Reformation. The Feast of the Madonna del Carmine is a fiesta for the whole of London's Italian community. It lasts several days, with the procession (Fig 17) as its highlight.

A little way to the east of the church is

16 Interior of St Peter's Italian Church, Clerkenwell Road.

the **Central School of Ballet**, formerly the Roman Catholic school of St Catherine Laboure, at which immigrant Italians learned English. It stands on the corner of former Little Saffron Hill, which was renamed **HERBAL HILL** in 1937 to recall the *Herbal* of John Gerard (1545–1611), the Elizabethan herbalist. He had a garden nearby in a spot then surrounded by woods, fields and meadows and containing about 1100 plants, which he catalogued in 1596. Tudor Holborn was a fertile area famous for its gardens, vines and herbs – remembered in the names of Vine Hill and Saffron Hill. Some of Gerard's plants came from the famous garden at Theobalds Park, Hertfordshire (cf. Theobalds Road, mentioned on p 18), where he worked as the superintendent for some 20 years. It was then the home of Lord Burghley, to whom Gerard (Fig 18) dedicated his *Herbal* in 1597. Herbal Hill here marks the borough boundary, its east side being in Islington. Nothing remains of the houses once colonised by Italian (mainly Neapolitan) craftsmen, or of the little RC church of St Peter & St Paul, opened here for their spiritual comfort by the energetic Father Kyne (p 42) in 1842.

Descend the hill to its junction with **RAY STREET**, known as Rag Street until blest with its present, less offensive name in 1774. Just around the corner to the right, at first-floor level, is a wordy tablet dated 1804, recording the parish boundary with St James', Clerkenwell. The boundary used to follow the river Fleet, which runs in a channel beneath us at this point. Across the street at **No.24** an iron shield marks the old border with the Borough of Finsbury, now the Camden–Islington frontier. At the far end of Ray Street,

17 One of the floats taking part in the procession during the Feast of the Madonna del Carmine.

beyond what is now Farringdon Road, was the original Clerk's Well.

Turn left (west) along Ray Street to the **Coach & Horses** pub, opposite the foot of Back Hill. The pub is a handsome 1900 construction in 'Queen Anne' style. We are now standing in what was known in the early 18th century as Hockley-in-the-Hole. Its name derived from the frequent overflowing of the Fleet river, 'hockley' being a dirty or muddy field in Anglo-Saxon. Suburban sprawl had reached this point by 1720, and it soon became a wretched locality, with rubbish tips towering over narrow back streets. Strype described it then as "a dirty place with some ill buildings . . . all very ordinary, both as to houses and inhabitants".

On the site of the pub stood an infamous Bear Garden, very popular in Queen Anne's day. A meander in the steeply-banked river provided a natural amphitheatre for such unsavoury spectacles as bear baiting, which in the 1690s moved from its old home at Bankside to Hockley-in-the-Hole; butchers (the principal patrons of the 'sport') gathered here from nearby Smithfield. From at least 1700 there were also combats in the 'noble art of self defence': wrestling, sparring matches and sword fights. Mrs Peachum in Gay's *Beggar's Opera* tells Filch that he must "go to Hockley-in-the-Hole, child, to learn valour". Mondays

18 John Gerard as depicted in his Herbal. *The Latin inscription reads "Portrait of John Gerard citizen of Cheshire and surgeon of London in the year of his age 53, 1598".*

and Thursdays were for bull and bear baiting, when animals were paraded solemnly through the streets. A 1710 advertisement is addressed to "all gentleman gamesters and others" for a dog fight and "a bull to be turned loose with fireworks all over him". A year earlier the

proprietor, Christopher Preston, was attacked and almost devoured by one of his beasts.

Flooding of the Fleet was not uncommon. In 1768 Hampstead Ponds overflowed, causing several thousand pounds' worth of damage in this area and among the courts of Saffron Hill. Several hogs were carried off and drowned. In 1846 a thunderstorm caused the Ditch to burst its banks, and there was severe flooding below Vine Street (p 46). In 1855 the Metropolitan Board of Works was made responsible for the Fleet, and a gigantic main drainage system was begun. In excavations for the great sewer to convey the river at a depth of about 13 feet below the surface, very close to where you are standing, workmen uncovered street paving stones worn smooth from over-use. Below the old street they came upon oak piles, black and slimy, the remains of a City mill dam, with wooden water pipes: the level had risen 13 feet in just over 200 years, probably from the accumulation of rubbish from the City after the Great Fire in 1666.

West of the Coach & Horses, Warner Street (p 52) begins. On its left side, and filling the entire block to the south, is a vast post-WW II electricity sub-station, once grandly dubbed 'Bankside House'; it covers a site acquired before the war by the County of London Electricity Supply Co. Here once lay the notorious Fleet Row, a self-contained enclave of street musicians. Charles Booth's 1889 poverty map marked this small area dark blue ("very poor, casual, chronic want"), and in places black ("vicious, semi-criminal").

Keeping to the *left* of the substation, turn south up still-cobbled **BACK HILL** as far as Summers Street. Ogilby's map of 1677 shows this as already developed, naming it as 'Hockley-in-the-Hole'; on the 1720 parish map it appears as 'Windmill Street' (cf. p 57), leading down to the river. Since the 19th century the 'Hill' has been the centre of the Italian community in London, and the heart of Little Italy.

As you walk up Back Hill, note the large utilitarian building on the left. Extending east to Herbal Hill, and occupying the site of an old timber yard, it was, until the 1950s, a warehouse, printing works and type foundry of Daily Mirror Newspapers. Called Reveille House, it presumably took its name from their once popular weekly. It has since housed departments of the London College (formerly School) of Printing, a part of the London Institute. Further up the hill, on the left at **No.4**, is the parish office of St Peter's, the starting point of the annual procession.

We, however, turn right into **SUMMERS STREET** (once Somers Street). On its south side, a furniture showroom, with lofts above, occupies a refurbished, white-painted **Winstone House**, once the printing works and printer's ink factory of B Winstone & Co. That this is Nos.1–10 explains the cryptic series of numerals on the façade. Long vanished from Summers Street are the mean Italian-occupied houses which in the mid-19th century, under the infamous slum landlord Thomas Flight, were regarded as especially insanitary. The *padrone* system (p 48) encouraged regional alliances, and the inhabitants of Summers Street were mainly Neapolitan. Their main occupation was organ grinding, a precarious, seasonal trade, bringing in from 9s to 14s a week (less than a general labourer's wage). Instruments were expensive, some costing as much as £25, so that most Italians hired them. In 1871, 46 organ grinders lived within 50 yards of each other in Summers Street, Eyre Place and Fleet Row (Fig 19).

We emerge into **EYRE STREET HILL**, which dates from about 1712, and whose narrowness towards the top reflects its original width throughout. The origin of its name is unknown; it was shown as Ayre Street on the 1720 parish map. The lower half of the hill was later known, until 1937, as Little Bath Street. (Great Bath Street, its northward continuation, which led towards the Cold Bath (p 53), no longer exists.) The painter George Morland (1763–1804) died in an Eyre Street Hill sponging house (a lodging house for those arrested for debt, prior to their trial before magistrates). He was overwhelmed by debt and neglect, and died in a "drunken delirium". The traditionally-fronted **Gunmaker's Arms** on the west side is a post-WW II successor to a beer-shop which had earlier thrived opposite, run by a succession of Italian families. Maybe its name recalls the nearby birthplace of the Maxim Gun (p 57). Further down the west side is a short terrace of surviving Georgian houses, including **No.31**, which still bears the sign of organ builders Chiappa & Co. Fig 20 (p 54) shows one of its employees punching holes in a roll corresponding to one of the tunes to be played. This firm survived the demise of manual operation of barrel organs by moving into the construction of fairground and cinema organs. Adjacent **No.33** was once home to both the Italian 'Unione Club' and the Knife Grinders' Union.

At the foot of the hill, turn left along **WARNER STREET** (once Great and Little Warner Streets). In July, during the annual fiesta (p 49), a *sagra* or fair is held here, featuring food and wine from all over Italy. As a sign still suggests, the street was wholly in the Borough of Finsbury until a 1965 boundary change placed its south side in Camden. Warner Street was originally a country path beside the river Fleet through Coldbath Fields, the property of Walter Baynes. The fields took their name from a cold bath, then London's best known, fed by a cold spring discovered by Walter Baynes, who exploited it for medicinal purposes. He advertised the water as "famed for the curing of the most nerval disorders". By 1720 John Warner of St Clement Dane's had purchased a joint share in the land, which he left to his son Robert in 1721. Robert Warner and Baynes divided the fields into building lots and leased them to Richard Baker, a St Pancras carpenter,

19 Drawing in The Graphic, *4 Sep 1875, entitled* An Italian colony in London; The organ grinders' quarters near Hatton Garden *(actually, Little Bath Street with Warner Street leading off to the right).*

who 3 years later built Warner Street and Baker's Row (the turning opposite the substation). Part of Coldbath Fields belonged to the Warner family until 1811. Henry Carey (born c.1690), the poet and musician who wrote *Sally in Our Alley*, lived and died in Great Warner Street. He was the illegitimate son of the Marquis of Halifax who had presented the Crown to William III and Queen Mary. Carey hanged himself here in 1743.

Warner Street is soon spanned by the viaduct of Rosebery Avenue (p 55). Before this, on the left, is Latchford's timber yard, a rare example of a traditional local trade still flourishing. From adjacent downward-sloping **WARNER YARD** (a truncated old Red Lion Yard), we have our first glimpse of Rosebery Square East (p 55), its rear elevation rising from, very nearly, the natural level of the valley floor.

Continuing under the viaduct, we reach the corner of **MOUNT PLEASANT**. Over the road to our right is the Mount Pleasant sorting office, at 7 acres the largest in Europe. The present building dates from 1926, but the Post Office first acquired the site in 1887. It had previously been occupied by the notoriously severe Coldbath Fields Prison, which opened here in 1794 and closed in 1877. The sorting office, and the eastern end of Mount Pleasant to our right, are in Islington; we turn left, keeping in Camden. The pub on the corner is the **Apple Tree**.

Although the building is Victorian, there has been a tavern of that name here since 1720. It was a favourite resort of prisoners discharged from the house of correction. It was once kept by a Mr Topham, 'the

strong man of Islington'. In 1741, to commemorate the taking of Porto Bello 2 years before by Admiral Vernon, he lifted 3 hogsheads of water weighing 1831 lb.

Beyond is a handsome row of houses

20 *Signor Ginocchio, who worked for Chiappa's, punching a musical text for a barrel organ, 1920.*

(**Nos.47–57**) which likewise date back to 1720. **Nos.47 & 49** retain their original appearance, with segment-headed window surrounds and parapets with dormer windows in mansard roofs. **Nos.51–53** were among the many addresses which once served O Comitti & Son, celebrated Italian barometer makers. At the far end of the row is a plaque marked *Dorrington Street 1720*, which is what this part of Mount Pleasant was called until 1884. The 1998 North London 'Pevsner' volume claims the plaque to be "not *in situ*", wrongly assuming it to have been brought here from present-day Dorrington Street (p 62). Westward is the site of another pub, the Cheshire Cheese, which once stood at No.61.

The name Mount Pleasant was first applied to the sloping triangular area, now paved and with benches, which we reach next. The course of the Fleet can readily be traced here, because war damage to the north exposed the natural contour of the land. Mount Pleasant was first so named about 1732, when the neighbourhood was developed, although it already had a bad reputation. It is almost certainly an ironic name, given that there was a huge laystall (tip) of cinders and rubbish on the river's banks (after which **Laystall Court**, on the left, was named).

Keeping to the left of the open area, turn south-east past the modern **Churchills** pub at No.79. Though

known as the Pillar Box when first opened, it stands on the site of an older tavern called the Two Blue Posts. On the left are **POOLE'S BUILDINGS**, once a row of Victorian tenements, but now only an access road. Walk up unlabelled **LAYSTALL STREET**. Though it probably took its name from the nearby rubbish tip, it was shown on early maps as Leicester Street. Strype commented that this street and others nearby comprised small brick houses chiefly inhabited by labouring men and the like. On the left we pass a Board of London School dated 1876. Closed by the ILEA, it served later as an adult education craft centre, until unusually reopened by Camden in 1996 as the Christopher Hatton Primary & Nursery School. Laystall Street was cut in half when Rosebery Avenue was built. Do not continue along its south-eastern half, but on reaching the busy main road, cross by the zebra crossing, and turn left along the latter's east side.

ROSEBERY AVENUE was constructed in 1889–92 under the auspices of the new London County Council, and was its first big achievement, opened by its Chairman, the 5th Earl Rosebery. It was also one of the last Victorian 'improvements'. Bridging the Fleet valley, and linking Theobalds Road with the Angel, Islington, it became an important tram route. Lining the road on either side are walk-up tenement blocks, attractively

refurbished by the St Pancras Housing Association. Built by James Hartnoll (p 72), and inappropriately named Rosebery Square, they were applauded by Charles Booth as a major advance in working-class housing. On the faces of both blocks are white plaques listing the names of erstwhile Clerkenwell vestrymen; they roughly mark the old border with St James' parish, which followed the line of the river, now many feet beneath us. Beyond, and visible opposite, just before the Warner Street bridge (and the present-day borough boundary), is another plaque, commemorating the wartime destruction and subsequent rebuilding of that end of Rosebery Square West.

Backtracking to the south-west end of Rosebery Square, turn left down steps into L-shaped **VINE HILL**, this leg of which was once called Bedford Street. The height of the steps gives some indication of the scale of the engineering works involved in constructing the Avenue. Vine Hill was probably the site of the vineyard of the Bishops of Ely (p 41), who paid workers 2d a day to harvest grapes. Ahead is a building with a castellated tower. On the brickwork facing up Vine Hill there are inscriptions

Ragged Schools and Refuges
Founded 1841 . . . Rebuilt 1877

This is where the Field Lane institution (p 42) moved to in 1878 after it was forced to leave Hatton Wall. The industrial schools later moved out to Hampstead.

In 1946 the building was considered too large for mission work, and the Field Lane Foundation retained just **No.16** Vine Hill as a Mission Centre. Its offices are still there. It now concentrates on helping elderly people by means of residential homes, and the homeless through a family centre in Mecklenburgh Square.

We ascend Vine Hill (here known as Vine Street until 1937) to the junction with **CLERKENWELL ROAD**, where we pause. On the corner is the **Duke of York** pub, the evening haunt in 1912 of Katherine Mansfield and Middleton Murry (p 72); dinner, for the cash-strapped lovers, usually consisted of a penny meat pie, washed down with a 2d pint of beer. The western end of Clerkenwell Road, to our right, was essentially a widening of existing Liquorpond Street. This dated from the 17th century, and probably derived its name from a brewery on its southern side. A brewery was certainly on the site of the present-day Bourne Estate (the council flats opposite) from 1693, when brewer Morgan Hinde acquired it. Strype wrote in 1720 that the brewhouse was "very large and gracefully built of brick". Richard Meux and Mungo Murray bought this brewhouse in 1757 and built a new Griffin Brewery, which became one of the largest breweries in London. By 1795 Andrew Reid, a rich City merchant, had joined Meux and together they set about building huge vats, which were then all the rage in the brewing world. A gargantuan vat, 60 feet in diameter and 23 feet high, holding 10,000 barrels, was erected at a cost of £5000. Two hundred people dined in it. An even bigger vessel, twice the size, was then erected, and was probably the largest in the world. In 1809, after disagreements between the partners, the business was reorganised, with Reid as the senior partner. Henry Meux moved to the Horseshoe Brewery in Tottenham Court Road. (The bursting of the vat there in 1814 curbed the rage for ever larger vats.) Andrew Reid died in 1841 but the firm prospered, until it was amalgamated with Watney and Combe. The brewery closed in 1899.

The **Bourne Estate** which is now on the site is an imaginative LCC development begun 1901–02, designed by W E Riley. Radcliff House facing Clerkenwell Road, and Redman House along Portpool Lane, form a continuous perimeter to the estate, pierced at intervals by archways which lead into a court in which stand six parallel blocks, interspersed with gardens. The solid brick-built blocks are six storeys high, containing flats and maisonettes under mansard slate roofs. The dwellings are served by access balconies, and single common staircases. The development was completed in 1908 and could hold 3900 people at high density on under 3 acres. The living-room and bedroom windows have unobstructed light but do not look onto the balconies, and are designed so that each tenement had at least one room overlooking the garden. The Bourne Estate was unique among schemes which the LCC completed before 1913 in having all the paraphernalia of Edwardian classicism. The LCC was very proud of it. The northern part of the estate was recently Grade II-listed.

Walk a few yards westward, noting opposite (on the Clerkenwell Road frontage of the Bourne Estate) two traditional shops, expressively named 'Clerkenwell Locks' and 'Clerkenwell Screws' – reminders of the area's long association with the ironmongery and hardware trades. Glance into the next turning on the right, where at **No.10 Laystall Street**, on the east side, Mazzini (p 37) set up a society for the advancement of Italian workers. It became the Mazzini–Garibaldi Club after Garibaldi visited Little Italy in 1864, and a commemorative plaque records this. West of Laystall Street are **Cavendish Mansions** (once Cavendish Buildings), model dwellings erected by Hartnoll (p 72) in 1882.

Now return eastward, and use the zebra crossing to reach the south side of Clerkenwell Road at its junction with Leather Lane. The Victorian warehouse on the corner (now offices) was long used by Gallaher's for the storage of tobacco and snuff. In medieval times Leather Lane ended here in a hill topped by a windmill, and the area was not surprisingly known as Windmill Hill. In the early Victorian period there was a pub at No.49 Leather Lane called the Windmill. In the 14th century Windmill Hill was also referred to as 'Le Hanging', and in Tudor times as 'Hanging Acre', which suggests that a gibbet stood here then.

Continue east, noting (opposite), a tiny access road labelled **WHITE BEAR YARD**. This is the last vestige of an old slum court, its name recalling a tavern which once stood nearby at No.1 Eyre Street Hill (p 52). On the corner of Back Hill, the antique dealers at No.142 have uncovered and retained the old fascia boards and trademark of former occupants W Lethaby & Co., makers of the 'LEDA' numbering machine.

Crossing Hatton Garden, look across at St Peter's Church, whose striking façade is better appreciated from this side of the road. Next door, to the left, is our final taste of Little Italy in the shape of an Italian grocer's: opened in 1890, it was run by the Terroni family until bought in the 1980s by Domenico Annesa of the Italian community in Bedford.

Buses for your homeward journey stop nearby. Alternatively, proceed to Route 5, which leads south from the Hatton Garden corner towards Chancery Lane station.

Route 5
Hatton Garden, Brooke's Market and St Alban the Martyr

This walk can either pick up from the end of Route 4 or start at a No.55 bus stop on Clerkenwell Road; or you can reach the starting point by a 5- to 10-minute walk from Farringdon station.

At the corner of Clerkenwell Road and **HATTON GARDEN** there are workshops named **Hatton House** (1880) bearing a blue plaque to Sir Hiram Maxim (1840–1896), inventor and engineer who designed and manufactured the Maxim Gun on these premises. His machine gun was perfected by 1884 and it could fire 600 rounds a minute. This house is No.57D, the strange numbering hereabouts resulting from the construction of Clerkenwell Road, when Christopher Street, as this top end of Hatton Garden had until then been known, was widened on its east side to align with Hatton Garden, which retained its original house numbers, ascending from Holborn Circus up to this point on the east side and continuing to rise on the west side all the way back to Holborn.

Keep on this side and cross over Hatton Wall. Directly opposite is a café, formerly the pub The Rose, as its floral pediment (painted black) attests. The building dates from 1899. Next door at **Nos.59–61** is Colonial Buildings, a large Victorian office block dating from 1881 in a debased but interesting palazzo style, red brick with carved stone and plaster surrounds. The huge square windows show that this must be an iron-framed structure. It is now home to various jewellery concerns.

On this side we pass the site (No.54) of a notorious police court, a dispensary of summary justice presided over by Mr Laing, the original of Mr Fang in Dickens' *Oliver Twist*, where Oliver was accused of stealing Mr Brownlow's handkerchief. The police court moved to Bagnigge Wells in 1842. Boyle's court guide of 1829 lists a Sergeant Sullen as residing here! The refurbished front of Sienna Buildings at **Nos.47–48**, a recent infill block, is enlivened with three gilt bas-reliefs of galloping horses put up in 1999.

Across the street Thomas Gainsborough (1727–88), the painter, was living during his apprenticeship in the late 1740s. On 15 July 1746, aged 19, he married Margaret Burr at Dr Keith's chapel in Mayfair, which was used for runaway marriages. She was the natural daughter of the Duke of Beaufort. He gave his residence as "in the parish of St Andrew's Holborn". The couple moved to lodgings in a house in Hatton Garden identifiable as No.67 (the site now buried under stone-faced New

House, built 1925). Their first child was probably the Mary Gainsborough of Hatton Garden whose burial was registered at St Andrew's, Holborn on 1 March 1748. Gainsborough's first painting on public exhibition was his view of the Charterhouse (Fig 21), presented in 1748 to the Foundling Hospital as one of the series of images of hospitals painted by British artists at Hogarth's behest. The Gainsboroughs left London early in 1749 to set up practice in Sudbury.

Upstairs at **No.67** is the Cartoon Art Trust, dedicated to the establishment of a museum in which British cartoon art can be permanently displayed. Behind No.67 was a coachyard giving on to No.36 Leather Lane, which runs parallel with Hatton Garden. In the late 18th century this was Felton's

21 Gainsborough's painting (1748) of the Charterhouse, one of the series of paintings of hospitals in London commissioned by Hogarth to hang in the Foundling Hospital, in part to demonstrate the work of British artists to potential patrons. Gainsborough, aged about 20 when he painted the picture, was just completing his apprenticeship to Gravelot and living in rooms in Hatton Garden with his bride Mary.

Coachworks. William Felton was a coachmaker who wrote a famous treatise on carriages in 1794; at the turn of the 19th century Leather Lane was known for its coach factories. His works were later associated with a historic ancestor of the motor car. Richard Trevithick (1771–1833)

CHARTER HOUSE.

had built the first successful steam carriage in Cornwall in 1800, but an improved version, his London Steam Carriage, was patented in 1802. It was built in Cornwall and then shipped to London, where it was fitted with a stage-coach body in Felton's Coachworks.

Its first run – and the first prolonged journey by a self-propelled vehicle – took it 10 miles from the coachworks on a round journey to Paddington and back via Islington. *En route* it was involved in London's very first motor accident, when it ran out of control and tore down 7 yards of garden railing. The London Steam Carriage failed to attract commercial backing and was broken up in 1804, Trevithick abandoning steam carriages for railway engines. In 1998 the engineer Tom Brogden made a faithful reproduction (Fig 22). It weighs 2 tons and carries eight passengers. It takes 20 minutes to fill the carriage's water barrels with 80 gallons, then 30 minutes to fire up the boiler to raise pressure to 30 lb per square inch – sufficient to budge the beast from a standstill. At idle the engine emits a slow snort which sounds like a horse and when it turns at 50 revolutions per minute it churns out 3 hp, enough to propel the car forward. The car has two gears, but three men have to turn the heavy 8-foot road wheels to align a driveshaft with a socket on the gearwheel. When all is in line a fourth man, in the driver's seat, pulls a lever to engage the gear. Braking is difficult – as demonstrated in the original vehicle's run.

Also across Hatton Garden, **Nos.69 and 70** are later-18th-century survivals; the latter, which turns the corner, is a well-proportioned four-storey house. On this side, on the near corner with St Cross Street, high up on the wall of **No.44**, is a tiny **plaque** put up in 1996 (the centenary of cinema) commemorating the early cinematographer Robert W Paul (1869–1943), who opened his first workshop here in 1891.

Crossing St Cross Street and noting the vintage postboxes at the corner (one early VR), we walk past a **handsome building** with large round-headed windows and white painted quoins, originally built as a small chapel in the mid-1680s. As the Hatton Estate (p 36) developed, the inhabitants needed a chapel. Wren was approached, but there is no evidence he had a hand in the design. The church was officially founded in 1696. Lord Hatton

hoped to enlarge it in 1711 after the Fifty New Churches Commission had been set up, but Hawksmoor thought it not strong enough. The residents of Hatton Garden petitioned again in 1717 for a Liberty that would extend to Brooke Street (this would

22 A 1998 reconstruction of Trevithick's London Steam Carriage of 1802, whose original bodywork was built in Felton's coachworks between Leather Lane and Hatton Garden.

have included 6000 people, enough to justify a minister), and the Churches Commission did draft an Act of Parliament in January 1718. But the church was surveyed and was not considered large enough.

It was converted in 1721 for use as a parochial school, which had previously been held in Brooke's Market (p 62), for 50 boys and 80 girls. The **figures** of two children in blue uniforms, identical with those outside the parish church of St Andrew's Holborn, were put up and can still be seen (they were evacuated to the country, like other Holborn children, during WW II and re-placed here after the war). The building, however, had to be rebuilt behind its façade after destruction in WW II, and is now used for offices.

Across the street is **New Garden House (No.78)** (1950s), a long imposing block with stepped mansard roofs, giant strip windows and Portland-stone cladding for the ground floor. This replaced a row of houses (Nos.71–83) gutted in October 1940. It covers the first site of the Foundling Hospital established in 1741 by Captain Thomas Coram (c.1668–1751), shipwright, master mariner and philanthropist (see *East of Bloomsbury*). The original intention was to use the house next to the chapel, but this proved too small and a lease was taken on a house opposite (No.73), formerly occupied by Sir Fisher Tench, and the house next door to

that (No.74). The Foundling Hospital paid rates on the two houses from June 1741 until September 1745. Work began in 1742 on a purpose-built hospital on 56 acres of Lamb's Conduit Fields, the boys moving out in 1745 and the girls in 1747.

Behind the original No.75 lay the Hatton Chapel, in Trinity Yard, reached via a passageway between Nos.26&27 Leather Lane. The Yards off Leather Lane were frequently associated with Nonconformists, as they provided secluded sites for chapels. 'Praise God' Barebones, who gave his name to Cromwell's 'Parliament of the Saints' and who was father of the rapacious developer Nicholas Barbon, lived on the north side of Holborn after the Restoration, and Baptist preacher Thankfull Owen died in Hatton Garden in 1681. Hatton Chapel was built in 1667 for a 300-strong Nonconformist congregation led by John Turner. In the 18th century it became a centre of Calvinistic Methodism. It was later known as Trinity Chapel, and was demolished in the later 19th century when Johnson Matthey expanded their premises.

The firm **Johnson Matthey** developed their gold and platinum business on this site from 1817, when Johnson rented No.78. By the 20th century its premises occupied Nos.73–83, taking up most of the land behind to Cross Street and Leather Lane. Johnson Matthey's was badly damaged by bombs in October 1940,

as were two houses next to it, No.72 (Langdale's Distillery of Essential Oils) and No.71 on the corner of St Cross Street (then a railway goods and ticket office). Langdale's was first situated on the south side of Holborn opposite Leather Lane, but was burned down in the Gordon Riots in 1780 at a cost of £100,000 and much loss of life. Johnson Matthey used to employ large numbers of workers before moving out to Southgate in 1976. In 1998 the firm sold the freehold of New Garden House for £21 million to the Prestbury Group. The HQ of Johnson Matthey's Precious Metals Division is still based in Hatton Garden, but across the road at **No.43**, next to the chapel.

Further along we pass **No.32**, now a rather faceless 1960s modernist building, whose back garden used to house public baths. Part of the house was let off to Samuel Plimsoll (1824–98) in the 1850s to run a small coal agency. Later an MP, he was responsible for introducing the load-line on ships. At **No.29** is Hatton Garden Pawnbrokers sporting a familiar sign, in an early-18th-century house with segmental window openings in rubbed small red bricks. Nearby is Minerva House (**Nos.26–27**), an early-20th-century classical block, refurbished in 1985 as offices for diamond dealers. No.27 was from the 1850s the City Orthopaedic Hospital, and the earlier building had some impressive Adam panelling, which was removed in 1907 and is now in the Victoria & Albert Museum.

On the opposite side, No.87 was until recently the London Diamond Club. Before that it was the last residential house of importance in the street, occupied by Sir Moses Montefiore (1784–1885), partner and brother-in-law of Baron N M Rothschild. Unfortunately, this fine house was being demolished at the time of writing, although its railings, whose tips bear pineapples at regular intervals, are being retained.

Reaching Greville Street, glance to the left and across the street at a row of 19th-century houses and jewellery shops with wooden attics in the roof. Now cross diagonally to the corner of Hatton Garden where, under the shadow of a tree, is a welcoming bench. Pause here and look across Hatton Garden at a row of interesting buildings. **No.23** with its prominent gable placed head-on to the street is a good example of late-19th-century Free Style, with an eye-catching round arch and a monogram, CPR, of the original business. It is all done in contrasting red brick and plaster work, sometimes called 'blood and bandages'. Past the old stuccoed front of **No.22**, we encounter **Nos.19–21**, the early-20th-century Treasure House, by Niven and Wigglesworth. It has a classical design with attached columns. The six stone carvings of seated figures on the façade

somewhat above eye level are sensitively detailed, and seem to represent four men mining, refining, fashioning and polishing precious metals for the adornment of two very satisfied women, one with a mirror.

We are about to leave Hatton Garden, but before we do let's recall some more of its residents and other associations. The Nursery Playhouse, a theatre and a training school for young actors, operated here in 1667–68: Pepys records performances of Shirley's *Constant Maid* in 1667 and Kyd's *Spanish Tragedy* in 1668. Early residents included George Bate (1608–69), physician both to Cromwell and to Charles II. He attended Charles I at Oxford and Cromwell in his last illness, then became principal physician to Charles II and FRS (his friends told Charles that he had poisoned Cromwell). In the 1670s William Wycherley (c.1640–1716), the dramatist, wooed the Dowager Countess of Drogheda who lodged here.

Now turn round, and walking to your left along **GREVILLE STREET**, note on the pink façade of **No.39 (Rajaveer Ltd)** two plaster oil jars. The building dates from the 1840s, and these are Camden's last remaining oil jars on a shop front (formerly customary for oil suppliers). On the corner of Leather Lane is a stuccoed 19th-century building surmounted by a blackened sign at parapet level inscribed "Pewter Platter 1876": this was a pub.

On reaching Leather Lane turn right

alongside the back of the Waterhouse Square development. As mentioned earlier (p 31) this new building covers part of Greville Street, and this had two important connections. First, the (later Royal) Free Hospital was established at No.16 from 1828 to 1843. William Marsden, a surgeon, had found a young woman dying on the steps of St Andrew's Church because she could not get admission to any hospital without a letter of recommendation from a subscriber. Marsden met members of The Cordwainers Company (the local landowner) in Grays Inn Coffee House (p 26) and they resolved to found the first hospital to admit patients without payment or a subscriber's letter of recommendation. The hospital opened on 17 April 1828 under the patronage of George IV. It has continued under royal patronage ever since. Officially called The London General Hospital for the Gratuitous Care of Malignant Diseases, it was familiarly known as the Free Hospital. In 1837 Queen Victoria decreed that henceforth it be called the Royal Free Hospital. There were only 30 beds in the rented house, but during the severe cholera outbreak in 1832 700 cholera sufferers were treated. In 1843 the hospital moved to a site in Gray's Inn Road, and is now in Hampstead. (Marsden also founded the Cancer Hospital (Free) in 1851, with sites in Fulham and Sutton, known as the Royal Marsden Hospital since 1954.)

The second important connection was at No.19, where the first London Co-operative Trading Association, part of the British Association for Promoting Co-operative Knowledge, was set up in the 1830s. On its first floor was a co-operative bazaar. William Lovett, who was a storekeeper on the ground floor, became Secretary of the British Association, and after the break-up of the London Co-operative Society in 1834 he opened a coffeehouse in Gray's Inn Lane for group meetings.

Follow the new building with its prominent Egyptian-style cornice round to the left into **BEAUCHAMP STREET**. The name is chiselled into the stone in a fashion that recalls how the street names were carved in terracotta in the original Prudential building. Beauchamp Street was named after Beauchamp Court in Warwickshire where Fulke Greville, Lord Brooke, was born in 1554. The white building opposite, **Beauchamp Building**, is a rather *art deco* design, recently refurbished to include a curved attic storey now let as expensive flats. Its entrance faces a neat little local authority block of flats, **Cranley Buildings** (1920s), in a vernacular style with mansarded gables. Beyond it the street opens out, right, into **BROOKE'S MARKET**, now a paved square with a few metal benches amid trees. The far side of the square is **DORRINGTON STREET**, first known as Dodington Street and shown as

such on Rocque's map of 1746, but corrupted to Dorrington Street by the turn of the century. Robert Greville, the last owner of Brooke House, married Ann Doddington [*sic*].

These three streets were laid out in the last two decades of the 17th century on the garden of Brooke House after its demolition. A small but popular open-air butchers' market was set up here by 1692 in a market house with stalls, although Strype says in 1720 that it "is of small resort as to the market but the shambles is pretty well served with meat". It was ruined when Smithfield became a dead-meat market in 1868. Just off Brooke Street to our left was once White House Yard, still existing in the early 1900s, with weatherboarded houses and a dairy where cows were milked.

The most striking building now is the five-storeyed, **cream-painted house** with bright blue wooden shutters to every window. This was designed by Halsey Ricardo, 1900–1910, and was for many years St Ursula's Hostel, founded in 1890 by Miss Florence Duncombe to provide a house of residence at moderate cost for young women under 30, daughters of professional men of small means who needed to study or work in London. Its ownership passed in 1985 to the St Pancras Housing Association. Above the entrance is a metal almond-shaped image of a crowned Virgin Mary sheltering

several saints in her veil.

In the far corner of Brooke's Market is the southern entrance to the church of **St Alban the Martyr**. Built in 1861–2 by William Butterfield in the Holborn slums, it was a successor to a chapel over a fish shop in Baldwin's Gardens and one in a cellar in Greville Street. The church was consecrated in 1863. William Henry, 2nd Lord Leigh (1824–1905) donated the site, and a tiny parish was formed which stretched between Leather Lane and Gray's Inn Lane, 500 yards by 200 yards, but containing 8000 people. John Gellibrand Hubbard MP (1805–1889), created Lord Addington in 1887, head of Hubbard & Co, Russia merchants in the City, and a former Governor of the Bank of England, financed the building. He wished to evangelise the area.

The handsomely decorated church (Fig 23) became a centre of 19th-century Anglo-Catholic Revival controversies. Prosecutions were brought for illegal ritual against the Rev Alexander Heriot Mackonochie (1825–1887), a Scot by descent but born in England and educated at Oxford, where he was imbued with the spirit of the Oxford Movement. Hubbard invited him to be the first curate. He had already stirred up trouble at St George in the East, where there were riots against his ministry in 1859. He always attracted huge congregations. He was suspended in 1870 after court action, and continuously hounded by the Church until he resigned in 1882, although he continued to work unofficially in the parish. Mackonochie is now considered by the Church of England to have been an important evangelical preacher. His centenary was celebrated in 1987.

Mackonochie was buried in Brookwood Cemetery, Woking, as were many of his parishioners and other Holborn inhabitants, taken thence by a special railway line, the London Necropolis Railway. This was an independent railway company, operating its own track by the side of Waterloo Station from 1870.

St Alban's rejoiced in a tall, aggressive design. Its 110-foot high saddleback tower has breadth, substance and authority, soaring above the surrounding LA housing. The body of the church (but not the attached neo-Gothic school and clergy house) was destroyed by incendiary bombs in April 1941 (Fig 24, overleaf), except for the saddleback tower, and was rebuilt by Adrian Gilbert Scott in 1961, who retained the tall space beneath the tower, as Butterfield intended.

Walk through the gatehouse. Suspended on the wall of the church ahead of you is a dramatic **torso of Christ** with arms outstretched. Entitled *Jesus Raised from the Dead*, it is by Hans Feibusch, 1985. It weighs 180 lb and is floodlit at night. Hans Feibusch (1898–1998) moved to London from Germany in 1933 after the Nazis banned and destroyed his works. He worked on many London churches and in the 1960s painted a 60-foot high mural of the Blessed Trinity inside the church. In the flagstoned yard beyond, with its two trees and flowers in pots, there is a glazed altarpiece within a rounded arched frame

23 Beautiful Victorian stone carving in St Alban the Martyr's (looking east), photographed in 1920.

of lemons and foliage, under a pantiled canopy. It is a Madonna and Child, white against blue, in the style of della Robbia.

Go into the church and admire its high, soaring vaulting. The site is hemmed in,

24 Interior of St Alban's, looking west, devastated by incendiary bombing in 1941.

and the east wall originally backed on to a tall tenement. Instead of a window, therefore, a large mural was used; the present one is by Feibusch. In the early 1930s St Alban's acquired a major reputation for music when the young Reginald Goodall (later famous as a Wagnerian conductor) was choirmaster, attracting the rich and famous, including Benjamin Britten, to concerts here.

Leave the church by the north entrance. Or, if this door is locked, backtrack through the yard and turn left past the former St Ursula's Hostel and left again through an archway marked *Fire Exit* along an unprepossessing alley way. This is **LEIGH PLACE**, named after the local landowner. It heads towards the modern yellow-brick building of **St Alban's Centre**, a social centre opened in 1992. A plaque records that the foundation stone was laid by Miss Edie Perry, a parishioner since 1907. In front of this is a block of flats called **Mackonochie House**, opened by the Bishop of London in 1994. The Church of England sold the land, which funded the new social centre, to St Pancras Housing Association, which built Mackonochie House for 'special needs' housing plus a mix of general family housing. It is in yellow brick with bright blue railings.

We are now in **BALDWIN'S GARDENS**. This was laid out in 1589 by Richard Baldwin (born c.1561), who combined the functions of Treasurer of Middle Temple (for 28 years) and Keeper of the Queen's Gardens. Exactly a century later Baldwyn Higgins, his descendant, sold the property to the ancestor of the Barons Leigh, whose family retained it until the 20th century. An early resident was Henry Coley (1633–c.1695), astrologer, mathematician and publisher of almanacs. Coley Street, to the north of Elm Street (p 72), was renamed in his honour. Baldwin's Gardens enjoyed some vague right of sanctuary for many years, and petty criminals fled here to live unmolested by the law until 1697, when an Act was passed which abolished the privilege of sanctuary both here and in many other places across London. The composer Henry Purcell (1659–95) escaped from his creditors here. It was not a very savoury place in the 17th century. In 1665 it was said that the 'common hackney prostitutes' of Baldwin's Gardens believed that VD gave them immunity from the plague.

Strype in 1720 calls it a large place, with a narrow entrance from Gray's Inn Lane, and "well built and inhabited, especially since new Buildings are raised in place of the old ones on the north side, where there is a handsome open square but not yet finished". Later, the area deteriorated and became a slum much frequented by criminals attracted by its narrow alleys and courts. Part of the locality was known as the Thieves' Kitchen, a training ground for young criminals. Henry Mayhew in the mid-19th century said the Kitchen was in Fox Court (a little to the south of Brooke's Court, see also p 75), although it may have been in Garden Court, site of St Alban's church. Mayhew, a journalist, highlighted the filth, dishonesty and immorality in lodging houses in this area which he said were unclean, uncomfortable and indecent, with sexes herded together indiscriminately and strong drink always admitted.

In the later 19th century this was a densely packed area, and working-class blocks used to stretch from here to Portpool Lane, which wartime bombing has now made visible across the wide open spaces (school and play areas). We can now see the back of the Bourne Estate (p 56) (the front of which is in Clerkenwell Road) abutting Portpool Lane, which we shall not actually traverse.

PORTPOOL LANE is a transference of the original name of Gray's Inn Road, but the street may cross the site of the ancient Manor of Purpool or Portpoole, once the property of the Canons of St Paul's. The manor was mentioned in a deed in 1262, when it contained pasture, ploughland, a dovecote and a windmill, and several lakes which have long since vanished. The street was developed in the 17th century. Strype in 1720 called it "a street of no great account, being old buildings, and none of the best inhabited".

Along Portpool Lane was built in 1850–51 one of the earliest blocks of working-class flats: the Thanksgiving Model Buildings, by the Society for Improving the Condition of the Labouring Classes and designed by the architect Henry Roberts. The block was so called because over £5000 was raised towards its construction in church collections on the Day of National Thanksgiving for deliverance from the cholera epidemic of 1849. It had accommodation for 28 families in self-contained one- and two-room flats and 64 rooms for 128 women.

Rents were only a shilling a week for the single rooms, a modest sum compared with the 4d per night commonly charged for lodgings elsewhere. It had a robustly classical composition with a banded base, massive arched elements for the staircases, and a crowning cornice. Putting the staircases in a giant arched recess was an idea taken up by Roberts for his model houses for Prince Albert and the Great Exhibition, afterwards re-erected in Kennington Park. An old building on the site was converted into a communal public bath- and wash-house, which was visited annually by about 20,000 people. The Thanksgiving Buildings were partially destroyed by wartime bombs and were taken down in the 1950s.

Walk left down Baldwin's Gardens to pass the north entrance of St Alban's (unless you have left the church by this door). Over the door are the words "Free For Ever to Christ's Poor", with an oblique reference to Hubbard's munificence in funding the church. Opposite is **St Alban's C of E Primary School**, rebuilt after the war in 1955 on the site of a former model school (1815) of the National Society (for the Education of the Poor in the Principles of the Established Church). It is now the only school in the area, and takes children from 3½ to 11. Visible to the north beyond the school, but not worth a detour, is **VERULAM STREET**, named after Francis Bacon (Baron Verulam) (p 68). Rose and Crown Court, whose site it covers, was home in the early 1670s to the author John Aubrey (1626–1697).

Continuing along Baldwin's Gardens, we soon reach Gray's Inn Road (p 74); turn left and in a few minutes you reach the Chancery Lane Tube station. Alternatively, cross the road and enter Gray's Inn (Route 6, overleaf).

Gray's Inn and adjoining roads

Take this circular walk between 12 and 2 on a weekday if you wish to walk or sit in the central garden of the Inn. But you may view the garden perfectly well during the hours when the gates are closed. The entire Inn is closed to the public at weekends.

Take the north-east exit ("Gray's Inn Road") from the Chancery Lane Underground station and walk up Gray's Inn Road for some 200 yards, to where an inconspicuous archway on the left leads into Gray's Inn. Here, in June 1780, the young Samuel Romilly (later Sir Samuel Romilly, noted criminal law reformer) stood sword in hand, with a trembling band of porters and servants behind him, ready to repel the Gordon rioters who were rampaging through the city. Either they were discouraged by Romilly, or they found more tempting targets elsewhere; in any event, they passed Gray's Inn by.

GRAY'S INN takes its name from Sir Reginald de Grey, justiciar of Cheshire, who leased what was then the manor or Portpool (or Purpool) from the dean and chapter of St Paul's in about 1294. It is tempting to link this acquisition by an eminent legal figure with the proclamation of Edward I in 1292 that only those properly trained should in future be permitted to plead in the King's Courts. But so neat a juxtaposition of cause and effect has not withstood the scalpel of modern scholarship, and it seems clear that the manor of Portpool did not become an 'inn' or *hospitium* for aspiring barristers until the third quarter of the 14th century. The lawyers took over the lease in 1395, but did not finally acquire the freehold until 1733.

Passing now through the archway into Gray's Inn Square, we note as we do so on the left a window of what was in the 17th and 18th centuries a bookshop; the grooves for the shutters can still be seen. **GRAY'S INN SQUARE** was built mainly in the last years of the 17th century, after most of the original buildings had been destroyed in a series of disastrous fires. The present buildings nevertheless look modern and for the most part are; Gray's Inn suffered terribly during the blitz, and the whole of the west and south sides of the square were lost. Some of the old buildings, particularly in the east side, remain. Mr Parker, solicitor to Mr Pickwick, had his offices here. Until 1685 a central east–west range divided the square into two halves, known as Coney and Chapel Courts; the origin of the former name is obscure.

On the south side of Gray's Inn Square lie the hall and **chapel**. Both were badly bombed on the night of 11 May 1941. The chapel seems to have been small loss. Although there had been a chapel on the site from the beginning of the 14th century, it was extensively rebuilt in the reign of James I, not a period distinguished for church architecture, and then 'gothicised' in 1826. After 1941 no attempt was made to rebuild it in its original form. Instead, a pleasant new chapel to a modern design was erected on the same site but extended eastwards to Gray's Inn Road. It was consecrated in May 1960.

The **hall** (entrance on the south side), by contrast, was rebuilt in 1950–51 just as it had been before the bombing (Figs 25, 26). The glass, pictures and other interior decorations had been removed to safety and were put back in place. The impressive hammerbeam roof required the wood from 160 oaks, not readily available in post-war Britain. The south oriel window was a gift of the American Bar Association. Most remarkably, the 16th-century screen was saved from the bombing by heroic efforts on the part of the firefighters, and is now also back in place. Legend has it that the screen was made of wood from one of the ships of the Spanish Armada, and modern research has confirmed that this may well be so; certainly, Lord Howard of Effingham, commander of the English fleet that fought the Armada, was a member of Gray's Inn.

The hall standing in 1941 dated mainly

from the time of Mary Tudor, and its reconstruction by Sir Edward Maufe (who also built Guildford Cathedral) is an intriguing if not particularly beautiful mixture of gothic and renaissance styles. The original purpose of the elaborate lantern in the roof (see Fig 25, also Fig 27 on p 69), was to carry away smoke from the fire burning on an open hearth in the centre of the hall – which was, incredibly, the only means of heating it until 1815, when an iron stove was installed. Although it had become redundant, the lantern was extensively reconstructed in 1826, and it is a replica of this that we see now.

In the 16th and early 17th centuries, the hall was the scene of many masques and other entertainments, generally built around the Christmas festive season. In 1594 a most elaborate masque, the *Gesta Grayorum*, was staged in which the 'Prince of Purpool' and his court underwent various allegorical adventures interspersed with dances and plays, including the first performance of Shakespeare's *Comedy of Errors*. The revelries lasted from 20 December to 6 January, and would have gone on longer had the authorities permitted. So professional was the performance that it was repeated before Elizabeth I a few weeks later.

The masque was revived in 1956 and

25 A 19th-century drawing of Gray's Inn Hall (the height of the roof exaggerated by the artist).

played before Queen Elizabeth II, who had been invited to visit the Inn for the purpose (Figs 28, 29 on pp 70, 71). The masque had been meticulously researched, and the producers had the advantage over their predecessors that it was no longer necessary for the female parts to be played by unbreech'd boys.

Past the hall, turn left into **SOUTH SQUARE** (originally Holborn Court), built in the 18th century but virtually obliterated in WW II. A particularly severe loss was the library, which had been opened only in 1929 and was a source of immense pride. Fortunately, the most valuable ancient books and manuscripts had been removed to safety. The South Square that we see now is post-war reconstruction; only **No.1** of the old houses is essentially intact. Dickens put David Copperfield's lawyer, Mr Traddles, in No.2. William Cobbett, the early-19th-century pamphleteer and champion of the poor, also worked as a young man in South Square; not surprisingly, he hated it.

The **statue** in the small garden in the

26 (Left) Gray's Inn Hall reconstructed after WW II, photographed in 1951 at its reopening.

27 (Right) Gray's Inn chapel and hall (from the north) in 1830, showing the elaborate lantern on the latter originally designed to take away smoke from a central fire in the Hall. The children visible in the drawing would be from families living in the Inn, as they do now.

centre of the court, erected in 1912, is of Sir Francis Bacon, Treasurer of Gray's Inn between 1608 and 1617 and perhaps its most famous member. Others include Henry VIII's minister Thomas Cromwell; Elizabeth I's ministers Nicolas Bacon (father of Francis), Lord Burleigh and Thomas Walsingham; Lord Howard of Effingham, of Armada fame; Charles I's Archbishop of Canterbury William Laud and, in our own time, Lords Birkenhead and Devlin.

Retracing your steps, head westward under an archway and past the Common Room (rebuilt in 1970) to **FIELD COURT**. The houses on our left are 18th-century survivals. To our right is a pair of impressive wrought-iron **gates** of 1723. The letters *T WIG*, set in the ironwork, recall William Gilby, the *Treasurer* of the Inn responsible for commissioning the gates. They lead to the equally impressive **gardens**, open to the public between noon and 2 pm. Originally laid out by Francis Bacon in the early 17th century (but substantially remodelled in the 1750s, allegedly by Capability Brown), they included a summerhouse which Bacon had had built for himself on the site of what is now No.4 Raymond Buildings (see later).

For some years the gardens were the haunt of rank and fashion. Samuel Pepys

was among the visitors and records in his diary for 4 May 1662 that he and his wife walked in Gray's Inn "to observe the fashions of the ladies, my wife needing some new clothes". However, as is so often

the way, the gardens were gradually taken over by rowdier elements. The benchers of the inn instructed the gardener to exclude 'ordinary people', but the decline continued. Women of the town began to

28 Dress rehearsal of Gesta Grayorum *in 1956.*

make their appearance, and the benchers eventually closed the gardens to the public. It seems a shame that, more than two centuries on, this magnificent open space is still open only for lunch-time picnics. Away to the right is a good view of **Verulam Buildings** (see also p 74), named after Sir Francis Bacon, whose titles included that of Baron Verulam.

If by chance you are there between 12 and 2 it is worth going up the Great Walk and looking at the remains of an ancient catalpa tree (a species of American bean-tree) on the left. Badly damaged in the gale of October 1987, it was according to legend brought to England by Sir Walter Raleigh and presented to Sir Francis Bacon. This time, modern research does not support the legend; the tree was probably planted a good deal later.

Continuing westward, we note on our left the modern (1964) **Inns of Court School of Law**. To our right, No.3 Field Court is a 1935 reconstruction. Turn right through another gate, and admire on your left an 18th-century building with elegant balconies decked out in pale blue. Our path now leads northward to Theobalds Road. On our right the modern **Atkin Building** merges harmoniously with the early-19th-century **Raymond Buildings** (named after the then Lord Chief Justice) which were allowed to encroach on the gardens and to swallow up the site of Bacon's summerhouse. Only a minority of chambers are let to barristers, others being occupied by various commercial and private tenants.

Authorities differ on the point, but the best opinion seems to be that it was at No.1 Raymond Buildings that the young Charles Dickens (he was only 14) came to work in May 1827. Although it must have been an improvement on the blacking factory where he had worked previously, Dickens did not enjoy his 18 months at Gray's Inn, and described it as "one of the most depressing institutions in brick and mortar known to the children of man". Confined as he was to a cramped office inadequately lit by cheap candles and piled high with dusty papers, it is perhaps not surprising that Dickens took a very different view of the Inn from that of the modern visitor come to admire the dignity and elegance of the ancient courts and gardens. Another gate gives access to the garden at the north end of Raymond Buildings.

We, however, leave Gray's Inn by the gateway to Theobalds Road and turn right along it, enjoying as we go a fine southward view across the gardens. Proceed to the next traffic lights, where stands a modest, typical late-Victorian police station, long disused, which has recently been re-acquired by Gray's Inn and is undergoing refurbishment and extension.

Intersecting here is **GRAY'S INN ROAD**, where we shall, for a short distance, turn left and north. Carefully crossing Theobalds Road, and passing the **Yorkshire Grey** pub, walk north up the west side of Gray's Inn Road (see also

29 Queen Elizabeth II eagerly awaiting the performance, as Elizabeth I had done in 1594.

71

p 74), observing the buildings on the opposite (eastern) side, which was fully built up by 1750. Early buildings included Stafford's Almshouses, recorded by Strype in 1720 as being for "6 men and 4 women"; they were demolished in the 1870s. Today the scene is dominated by the red-brick mansion flats of the Hartnoll Estate. Speculative builder James Hartnoll erected some 4,000 'industrial dwellings' in various parts of London, as well as a number of mansion blocks. They were built on land he bought cheaply (and controversially) from the Metropolitan Board of Works in the wake of its road-improvement schemes. Between 1885 and his death in 1900, the Southwark-born former joiner amassed a sizeable fortune, leaving £440,000 in his will. Here, in a then recently widened Gray's Inn Road, he built turreted **Tiverton Mansions** and its companion, **Dawlish Mansions**. The Hartnoll family hailed originally from North Devon, hence the Devonian names. **Dulverton Mansions**, to the north and with curly 'Dutch' gables, was originally named Clovelly Mansions.

So too, confusingly, was a further block beyond Elm Street, now known as **Churston Mansions.** Here in 1912 lived short-story writer Katherine Mansfield. "Make me your mistress" was her invitation to the future writer and critic, John Middleton Murry, who abandoned his Oxford studies to join her here in her "tiger's lair". Minimally furnished, and with brown packing paper on the walls, Flat 69 doubled for 4 months as a love-nest and as the editorial office of *Rhythm*, the avant-garde review which the couple co-edited.

We have now reached the former boundary with St Pancras; for Gray's Inn Road north of this point, see *East of Bloomsbury*. Using the zebra crossing, turn east down **ELM STREET**; its name is said to derive from a row of elm trees which once ran down to the river-bank hereabouts. The street lies roughly on the line of an old Rope Lane, which Strype described (in 1720) as "broad and dirty, not paved, with poor houses on the north side". The worst nightmare on this Elm Street occurred on the night of 21/22 March 1944, when the same north side was ravaged in the final raid of the 'Baby Blitz'. An ugly 1960s office-block sprouted here at **No.10**. As 'Elm House' it was the unlikely home of the *Illustrated London News*; re-clad in grey, it now houses the Serious Fraud Office.

Opposite, on the site of what was once Fleur de Lys Court, is **Holsworthy Square**, model working-class dwellings of 1890 built around a courtyard by James Hartnoll (see above). Rundown by 1980, the 'square' was acquired by the St Pancras Housing Association, along with other Hartnoll blocks, and refurbished 6 years later.

At the bottom of Elm Street, turn right, and keeping the Churchills pub (p 55) well to your left, veer right to pass between the post-WW II council flats of **Mullen Tower** and, on the right, the studios and workshops of **Panther House**, formerly Lever's optical equipment factory. We now venture along what is now the south-east end of **MOUNT PLEASANT** (see also p 55). From the broad street it was on the valley floor, this is suddenly transformed into a narrow, winding lane. Originally known as Little Gray's Inn Lane, this ran by 1818 through a 'mini-rookery', noted for its brothels and gambling dens, and inhabited by Irish families sleeping 8 to a room. At the first right-hand bend, an equally narrow Tothill Street once struck east to join Laystall Street (p 55). In 1871 it contained a piano factory, and boasted among its residents an Irish leech dealer. The street was obliterated in the building of Rosebery Avenue. Looming now on the left is the grim rear of Gray's Inn Buildings (p 74). Opposite is the site of the even grimmer Holborn Union Workhouse, which in Victorian times extended northward towards Elm Street. The workhouse was sketched (Fig 30) by local antiquarian and topographical artist, John Philipps Emslie (1839–1913). For nearly 50 years he lived directly opposite at 47

30 Stafford's Almshouses and Holborn Union Workhouse (J P Emslie, 1874).

Gray's Inn Road. Emslie undertook for the Topographical Society of London to draw "buildings recently either doomed or demolished". The workhouse was replaced by 'The Hostel', an LCC facility for transients, of which the Camden Council premises near the far end of the lane are a vestige.

Turn left at the end, then left again at the lights to observe the western extremity of **CLERKENWELL ROAD** (see also pp 46 & 56). Immediately ahead lies its acute-angled junction with Rosebery Avenue (p 55). Here **Burlington's** beauty salon not only occupies the corner site, but

VIEW OF STAFFORD'S ALMSHOUSES AND PART OF THE EAST SIDE OF GRAY'S INN ROAD: drawn by J. P. Emslie

has also recycled an adjacent Victorian underground public convenience. Cross there to the south side of Clerkenwell Road, where the **Griffin** pub, an offshoot of the once adjacent Griffin Brewery (p 56), stands next to modern **Gray's Inn House** at No.127, the latest home of the London Weather Centre (see also p 23). Look across to the north side of the road, where the block to the left, on the corner of Gray's Inn Road, is decorated with a number of river-god reliefs. Occupying a ground-floor shop is the ***Scuola Guida Italiana***, an Italian driving school (we are here on the western fringe of 'Little Italy', see Route 4). To the right, and extending back along Rosebery Avenue, stand **Gray's Inn Buildings**. Built as model dwellings by the Artizans & Labourers General Dwelling Co., they were known at first as Gray's Inn Residences. Later acquired by Holborn Borough Council, the flats have latterly been let by Camden as short-life tenancies. Ostentatiously adorned with a long series of bold lion's head reliefs, they might be mistaken for an old civic hall.

Back on the south side, and rounding the corner into **GRAY'S INN ROAD**, is the site of the real thing. An uninspiring 1960s office block, known rather grandly as **Holborn Hall**, commemorates the old town hall, built in 1878 in Italianate style (see front cover) and boasting a conspicuous clock tower with four faces

none of which, if contemporary accounts are to be believed, ever told the correct time. Despite having been built on a lavish scale, with a meeting hall licensed to hold 900 people and two concert halls, it remained the town hall for barely 30 years. It was supplanted as town hall by a building that stands on the south side of High Holborn, but west of Kingsway and therefore outside the area dealt with in this book.

Returning to the crossroads, cross very circumspectly to the other side of Gray's Inn Road, and turn down the western side towards High Holborn. This was originally known as Portpoole Lane, as it led to the manor of Portpoole, in which Gray's Inn was founded (see p 66). From the 14th century until 1862 it was known as Gray's Inn Lane. The stretch of it where we are now standing was built up by 1570 and was described by Stow in 1598 as "furnished with fair buildings and many tenements on both the sides leading to the fields towards Highgate and Hamsted". 17th-century residents of the street included the dramatist James Shirley (1596–1666) in the 1630s and the parliamentarian John Pym (1584–1643) in 1640.

In the 17th and 18th centuries Gray's Inn Lane was one of the main thoroughfares entering London. Down it came General Monk in 1660 to restore the monarchy, and down it too came the eponymous hero in Henry Fielding's *Tom*

Jones. In the 18th century the buildings were still mostly half-timbered; Strype wrote that the east side had a great many courts and alleys with narrow entrances. It was not primarily residential, but full of shops and inns. From about 1738 to 1767, one very fine shop belonged to Thomas Osborn, London's leading dealer in old books. In 1742 he bought the library of Edward Harley, Earl of Oxford, but sold it 2 years later and thus missed the chance of becoming one of the founders of the British Museum.

The street was only 30 feet wide south of the Theobalds Road crossroads, and this became increasingly inadequate for the traffic it carried. In 1877 the Metropolitan Board of Works secured powers to widen it, and the work was completed in March 1884. In the process, all the remaining wooden buildings were demolished, including slums behind, which were replaced by model blocks for working men known as Baldwin's Buildings. A satirical piece in the *Holborn Guardian* of 22 March 1889 described a procession at the opening of the widened Gray's Inn Road. The procession led to the new town hall (where those marching were to enjoy a feast) and included a "posse of the late residents of Fox Court, Baldwin's Gardens and other slums, six abreast, all in their native costumes and war paint".

Walk south down Gray's Inn Road. On our right, behind a high brick wall, rises the façade of **Verulam Buildings** (see also p 71), part of Gray's Inn, built between 1803 and 1811. Totally devoid of decoration, the buildings represent the last gasp of Georgian severity. Either the benchers of Gray's Inn were old-fashioned, or they just wanted the job done on the cheap. If the gate is open, venture inside. Here, as elsewhere in the Inn, the buildings' date of construction and the commissioning Treasurer's initials are recorded on keystones over the doors. The *T SR* legends at **Nos.1–3** commemorate the illustrious Samuel Romilly (p 66), Treasurer of the Inn in 1803.

On the opposite, east, side of Gray's Inn Road some Victorian buildings from the road widening of 1877–1884 have survived the Blitz and subsequent redevelopment. **No.54** has since 1987 been the home of the AIDS charity the Terrence Higgins Trust. South of Baldwin's Gardens (p 64) look up **BROOKE'S COURT** to the view of St Alban's and its imposing tower (p 63). This is the only survivor of the maze of little courts and alleys which once covered the area. Until 1937 it was called Bell Court, and had been formed out of the yard of a Bell Inn which stood just outside the garden wall of Brooke House (p 28). The inn is shown on Ogilby's map in 1677, but Bell Court had been laid out by 1720 when Strype called it "a very handsome large place with a freestone pavement"

surrounded by new, brick-built buildings. It deteriorated thereafter, and the area was a slum by the turn of the 19th century.

Beyond Brooke's Court, virtually the whole of the east side of Gray's Inn Lane fell victim to comprehensive redevelopment in the mid-1970s: a variety of small shops, including an off-licence, a restaurant and a much-loved florist's were swept away, to be replaced by glumly unimaginative office blocks. Perhaps among the latter we may make an exception for the dark-glass-fronted building with a railinged ramp at **No.14**. Anonymous and strangely sinister, it is allegedly devoted to the black arts of information technology. It provides a strong contrast to the Tudor buildings of Staple Inn in front of us.

The redevelopment of the 1970s totally eliminated Fox Court, an alley beside whose entrance the Fox alehouse once stood. In this alehouse was born an illegitimate child who grew up to be the poet Richard Savage (1697–1743); his mother, Anne Countess of Macclesfield, wore a mask throughout the birth to disguise her identity. Savage lived a dissipated life, haunting London's fleshpots with amongst others his friend Dr Johnson, who wrote a well-known biography of Savage. He often attacked his alleged mother, for instance in his poem *The Bastard* (1729). Condemned to death for murder after a tavern brawl, he was

pardoned, but died in a debtors' prison at Bristol.

The Fox was also the headquarters of the Cato Street Conspiracy (1820) – a plot to murder Castlereagh and other cabinet ministers and in the ensuing confusion to proclaim a provisional government which, it was hoped, would then lead to a general uprising. The plot was inevitably betrayed (indeed, it has been suggested that it was formed on the initiative of a government *agent provocateur*) and its leader, Arthur Thistlewood, and his co-conspirators were arrested in Cato Street (off the Edgware Road) and duly hanged.

At the south end of Gray's Inn Road we are back at the Chancery Lane Tube station, where this walk began. If you wish, cross High Holborn and proceed westwards to the corner of Chancery Lane, where Route 7 around Lincoln's Inn begins.

Lincoln's Inn and adjoining roads

This walk is best undertaken on a weekday, as Lincoln's Inn is closed to the public at the weekend. The walk starts at the eastern corner of Chancery Lane and the south side of High Holborn, some 70 yards west of the Chancery Lane Tube station.

The boundary between Camden and the City runs down the centre of Chancery Lane. We shall therefore ignore the buildings on the eastern, City, side, but it is best to walk down that side of the street in order to have a good view of the buildings opposite. The only building in the Lane we shall note for the time being is **No.76**, an exotic Victorian confection of different styles. Until recently it was the rather improbable home of the London offices of the Xinhua news agency of the People's Republic of China. Then, past a narrow alleyway, Stone Buildings (p 79) of Lincoln's Inn appear.

Your stance on the City pavement gives you a good view of the replica Elizabethan chimneys and lion-head rainwater spouts within the Inn. Ignore the wide gap leading into the Inn by the side of Stone Buildings (adequate for motor vehicles, though they are not encouraged), and continue until you come to an ancient oak gateway surmounted by three coats of arms. This is the old gatehouse to **LINCOLN'S INN**, and the coats of arms are of Henry VIII, who was king at the time, the Earl of Lincoln, reputed founder of the Inn, and Sir Thomas Lovell, who had fought at Henry Tudor's side at the battle of Bosworth and was a major benefactor. It was probably through this gatehouse that in 1832 the Duke of Wellington took refuge from a mob that was pursuing him to express, in forcible terms, its opinion of the Duke's opposition to the Great Reform Bill. The gatehouse dates from 1518, but it was damaged during the war and had to be rebuilt in the 1960s. The oaken door itself dates from 1564.

The origins of Lincoln's Inn are a matter of controversy. It is not even known for certain whether the name comes from the Earl of Lincoln, a major legal figure in the closing years of the reign of Edward I, or of one Thomas de Lincoln, a serjeant-at-law, around whom there grew up a school of what might be called legal apprentices in the mid-14th century. The tradition of a connection with the Earl of Lincoln is strong, and has some supporting evidence, but if he did found the Inn it was a very early foundation indeed, since the Earl died in 1311. What is certain is that by the time contemporary written evidence becomes available with the commencement of the famous Lincoln's Inn "Black Books" in 1422 (the oldest written sources of any Inn), the Inn was established on its present site on land leased from the Bishop of Chichester. The freehold was purchased in 1580.

Lincoln's Inn has had its full share of famous members. Pride of place must perhaps go to Sir Thomas More, Lord Chancellor under Henry VIII but later executed for refusing to accept Henry's headship of the English church. There is a strong tradition that Oliver Cromwell studied for a short time at Lincoln's Inn, though proof is lacking. No fewer than fifteen prime ministers have been members, including Disraeli, Gladstone, Thatcher and Blair. William Pitt the younger (1759–1806) was made a bencher at the tender age of 23, when he was already Chancellor of the Exchequer. His turn as Treasurer came in 1794 (the office of Treasurer, the most senior in the Inn, is held by the benchers in rotation), and is commemorated by a sundial on the west wall of Stone Buildings erected on the site of his chambers and bearing the initials *W P*. As the sundial is shut off from the morning sun its hours run only from 1 to 8. The Inn can also claim the first Jewish barrister (1833) and the first woman bencher (George V's widow Queen Mary in 1943 – admittedly, her post was an honorary one).

Passing through the gateway, we find

ourselves in an almost completely enclosed courtyard with the Old Hall in front of us and the chapel to our right; the only gap in the buildings is a narrow passage between the chapel and the chambers fronting Chancery Lane. (For orientation, see the aerial view of the Inn, Fig 31.) Behind us above the gateway are three more coats of arms: of John Hawles, Treasurer in 1695, of Lord Upjohn, Treasurer in 1965 (when the gateway was being reconstructed), and – slightly unexpectedly – of Princess Margaret, who is an honorary bencher and was Treasurer in 1967 when the work of reconstruction was completed. Here and elsewhere it is the custom of the benchers of Lincoln's Inn, as at Gray's Inn, when work needs to be done on the fabric of the buildings, to commemorate the fact with a plaque containing the initials of the Treasurer of the day and the date.

The courtyard in which we stand, known as **Old Buildings**, was built and rebuilt at various dates between 1524 and 1609, though there has been some reconstruction in modern times. The **Old Hall** is even older, being built originally between 1489 and 1492 (Fig 32) to replace the original hall of the Bishop of Chichester; it was extensively rebuilt in the

31 Aerial view of Lincoln's Inn, drawn by an unknown artist about 1930. How he obtained his vantage point is a mystery. Note the proximity of the Inn to the Law Courts.

77

1920s. In the 18th and 19th centuries, up until the opening of the Royal Courts of Justice in the Strand in 1882, it was the seat of the Court of Chancery, and it was here that the interminable lawsuit of Jarndyce vs. Jarndyce in *Bleak House* was played out. Charles II visited on at least four occasions, and it seems that on his last visit in 1672 his hosts became so drunk that the King excused them from standing to drink his health. Whatever the truth of this story, the members of Lincoln's Inn certainly have the privilege of drinking the loyal toast seated and have exercised it, including on the occasion when Queen Elizabeth II and the Duke of Edinburgh came to dine in 1967.

To our right, the **chapel** was rebuilt between 1619 and 1623 (the west bay being added in 1882), deliberately in medieval style to match the other buildings in the Inn. We must dismiss (as Pevsner does) an attribution to Inigo Jones: it is inconceivable that he would have lent his name to a building in such a style. The opening sermon was preached by John Donne, poet and Dean of St Paul's; it was said that the crowd was so great that several people fainted in the crush. In the mid-19th century the chapel became a centre for Christian Socialism when F D Maurice was appointed chaplain. The benchers of Lincoln's Inn appear to have been more tolerant than the authorities of King's College, London, who dismissed

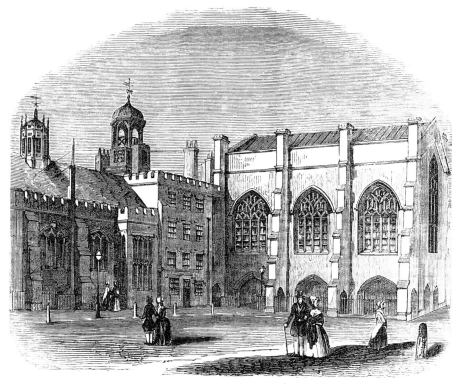

32 Lincoln's Inn Old Hall and Chapel (note the undercroft under the latter), featured in the October 1844 Supplement to The Saturday Magazine. *The 'belvedere' visible in this and other contemporary drawings to the right of the Hall was actually a clock tower rising above the range of buildings between Hall and Chapel erected early in the 19th century but demolished in 1883.*

him from the Chair of English literature because of his unorthodox views on the subject of eternal punishment.

The chapel is built above a fine undercroft which seems to have been intended to enable members to take the air on rainy days; at least, Pepys records it as being used for that purpose. In the 18th century it became a favourite place for unmarried mothers to leave their unwanted babies. Until 1750 the Inn would offer five shillings per baby to anyone prepared to take them off their hands, but after that date the Inn adopted them, gave them the surname Lincoln, and saw them apprenticed to useful trades (or, no doubt, service in the case of the girls).

In May 1659 a clandestine meeting of ex-members of the Long Parliament was held in the undercroft to discuss the possible restoration of Charles II. The meeting was at the initiative of one of the Inn's more colourful members, William Prynne, who managed the considerable achievement of being imprisoned by both Charles I and Cromwell. An extreme puritan, Prynne had an almost pathological hatred of Jews, Catholics and life's pleasures, in broadly equal proportions. It was a diatribe against the theatre that first aroused the ire of Charles I (his queen was fond of amateur theatricals, and Prynne's broadside was interpreted as an attack on her). Prynne was ordered to be put in the pillory and have his ears cut off,

and Lincoln's Inn dutifully expelled him from membership. But this did not stop him from writing, and 3 years later he was convicted again of seditious libel and sentenced to be branded, imprisoned and "to lose what remained of his ears". Released by the Long Parliament, Prynne was restored to his place in Lincoln's Inn, became a bencher in 1647 and a Member of Parliament the following year. But he soon came to the view that the tyranny of Cromwell was no better than that of Charles I, and by 1650 he was in prison again. This time his Inn seems to have stood by him, for he was Treasurer in 1657 and as already noted he later worked there actively for the Restoration. A grateful Charles II gave him a sinecure, and on his death he was buried in the undercroft. "A good honest plain man" said Pepys, with some understatement.

In 1990 it was proposed to glaze in the undercroft so that it could be used for receptions (with an eye, perhaps, to weddings held in the chapel above). The proposal was vetoed by the planning authorities: its architectural incongruity aside, it was felt wrong to permit social events which might include dancing on what had until the mid-19th century been used as a place of burial.

Squeeze now between the chapel and the Old Buildings, and you find yourself in **OLD SQUARE**, a pleasant if not particularly inspired late-Victorian

composition built between 1874 and 1887, mostly by the prolific Sir George Gilbert Scott and his son. The square was the target of one of history's earliest air raids when a bomb fell on it in 1915, damaging the chapel and killing a passer-by. On 18 December 1917 another bomb fell outside the Yeomanry entrance (see below); deep shrapnel pits can still be seen in the walls of buildings over a wide area.

Continue north past the vehicle entry from Chancery Lane, and you have a fine view of the elegant **Stone Buildings**, designed by Sir Robert Taylor and built mainly between 1775 and 1780. There are in fact three distinct blocks. On the Chancery Lane side is a brick range with a stone section in the middle. The latter originally housed the Clerks to the Court of Chancery, whose status was regarded as entitling them to a building of stone rather than brick. When the Court of Chancery moved to the Strand in 1882 their offices at **No.10** became the headquarters of the Inns of Court Volunteers, and still houses that body's successor regiment, the Inns of Court and City Yeomanry. The second block, filling the north and most of the west sides of Stone Buildings, is a handsome uniform range intended for barristers' chambers. It just fails to join up with the east range, and between the two an alleyway too narrow for any but pedestrians leads to Chancery Lane – a curiously inconsequential piece of planning. Finally, at the south end of the west range is an imposing addition built in classical style in 1842–5 by Philip Hardwick, who also built the New Hall and library (see below); it was Philip Hardwick who was responsible for the much lamented Euston Arch.

Retrace your steps now and go back to Old Square. The 19th-century **New Hall and library** stand in splendid isolation across the grass to the west, on the edge of Lincoln's Inn Fields. The limitations of the site no doubt account for the curious L-shaped configuration, with the hall to the south, the library athwart it to the north, and a council chamber and other administrative rooms in between. During legal terms, which were short, the Court of Chancery used to sit in Westminster Hall, but out of term in the Old Hall at Lincoln's Inn. The need for a new hall and library arose respectively from the inconvenience of the Court of Chancery sitting in the old hall, and the proliferation of law books when legal business increased in the first half of the 19th century. For the new buildings Hardwick chose a Tudor gothic ('Picturesque') style which was then much in vogue. The new hall and library were completed in 1845 (though the library proved inadequate and had to be enlarged to the east in 1871–3); "an eminently successful piece of Romantic design", says Pevsner approvingly. Queen Victoria and Prince Albert were invited

to the banquet held to celebrate, and it is recorded that when Prince Albert's health came to be drunk Victoria enthusiastically drained her glass to the bottom.

To our left (south) is another small courtyard of early-Tudor buildings. Beyond it opens up the spacious expanse of **NEW SQUARE**. Begun in 1680 as a speculative development by a member of the Inn named Henry Serle, who owned the land abutting Lincoln's Inn Fields, its administration was after complex negotiations taken over by the Inn, and the square was completed in the early 1690s by the ubiquitous Nicolas Barbon, who built so much and so shoddily around the area of Red Lion Square. It seems that for once Barbon did a good job, for apart from bomb damage the square has survived almost untouched to this day. Despite the 19th-century date on it, the imposing arched exit to Carey Street in the south-east corner is part of the original design.

The complexity of the agreement between the Inn and Henry Serle was in no way eased by Serle's inconveniently dying intestate and his eventual heirs becoming bankrupt. The Court of Chancery ordered that the leases on the chambers be sold, thereby creating a network of 'flying freeholds' (so called because the owners of the chambers did not own the land above which they were built), which proved such an administrative nightmare

that the management of the square eventually (1860) had to be regulated by a special Act of Parliament. Today most, but by no means all, of the freeholds are owned by the Inn.

New Square is not symmetrical. The west side runs further north than the east side, and between the east side and the extension to Old Buildings there is a set of railings bearing the date 1928, within which is a small garden. This was once the site of the Inn's herb garden, and in 1995 it became one again. The wall of **No.1 New Square** is forbiddingly blank, and a notice dated 1693 proclaims that "no windows to be broken out without leave". The wall contains no fewer than nine bricked-up windows. The window tax was not introduced until 1696, but perhaps the benchers had early warning of its impending arrival. Dickens worked for a few weeks as a clerk in No.4 New Square before transferring to Gray's Inn (p 71).

At the Chancery Lane end of the garden stands the modern **Hardwicke Building**, let as barristers' chambers or private flats. Further south, and approached by a separate footway, stands another new building inserted between New Square and Chancery Lane. A foundation stone announces that it was laid by Sir Michael Carr on 20 December 1989 and adds disarmingly that it stands "on the site of communal privies 1693–1987 always known as the boghouse". This building was ancient enough to be listed, and its demolition aroused a good deal of controversy. Unlike other public lavatories it was divided into three rather than two parts, labelled respectively *Ladies, Benchers* and *Members and Tenants*; what you did if you fell into none of these categories is not clear. Formerly, men could leave the Inn through the gate by the Hardwicke Building and pass into Star Yard (now approached solely from Carey Street, see below) to use the cast-iron urinal abutting the Inn wall; the structure is still there, but is no longer in use.

At the other, western, end of the square is the gateway into Lincoln's Inn Fields built by Philip Hardwick's son to harmonise with the New Hall. Continue south, however, to leave the Inn by the archway within which the law bookseller **Wildy's** ("since 1830") is worth a glance for its eccentrically displayed prints of local interest.

Turn right into **CAREY STREET**. Its name, which recalls that of a householder here in the early 17th century, became a euphemism for bankruptcy ("He's in Carey Street"), the bankruptcy court having once been situated here. Henry Mayhew, one founder of *Punch* and author of *London Labour and the London Poor*, began work as a clerk in his father's Carey Street law office, "very little to the satisfaction of any of the parties

concerned". Beyond a photocopying shop the tiny **Silver Mousetrap**, "Established 1690", graces the north side of this little street. Further west comes the **Seven Stars** pub, claiming a 1602 start date.

33 Watkins, clockmakers, at 51 Carey Street, "one of London's smallest shops", celebrating its centenary in 1951. The Wig Shop now occupies the site.

Next comes another tiny establishment at No.51, The Wig Shop, selling (guess what!) barristers' wigs, where in 1951 Watkins, the clockmakers, celebrated the centenary of its foundation (Fig 33). Beyond it there is yet another entrance to Lincoln's Inn, dated 1888. Finally we encounter the **Sir Thomas More chambers** on the corner of Lincoln's Inn Fields, with a statue of the man of high integrity at first-floor level.

Cross Carey Street, even though this takes you into Westminster, and return eastwards to admire the late-18th-century house (**No.60 Carey Street**) on the western corner of **STAR YARD**, at one time used as the official residence of the President of the Law Society during his one-year term of office, but now converted to offices. A handsome classical building stretching from Star Yard to Chancery Lane was built in the 1860s as the premises of the Union Bank of London (see **Union Bank Chambers** at its western end). Taken over first by the National Provincial and then by the National Westminster before finally closing its doors in 1996, the eastern end has recently been converted into a restaurant, named **The Knights Templar**, with full use made of the ornate decoration of the banking hall.

Turn left into **CHANCERY LANE**, probably built by the Knights Templars to lead from the Temple to fields they owned to the north. Give a passing bow to

Ede and Ravenscroft at **Nos.93-94**, who have been selling wigs and robes to the legal fraternity since 1689. Next door at **No.92**, Bridge the stationers retains an pleasant shop front. Glance briefly into **CHICHESTER RENTS**, an attractive alleyway now lined with shops and sandwich bars – a welcome relief from the serious pursuit of legal and commercial matters to which Chancery Lane is otherwise devoted. The Bishops of Chichester, who frequently filled the office of Lord Chancellor through the 13th and 14th centuries, originally had a palace here. The shops include a coffee bar, where you may pause for refreshment before proceeding north past **BISHOP'S COURT**, named thus for the same reason, but consisting now only of a dreary alleyway. Next, **No.78**, now a wine merchants, was for more than 100 years the site of Chancery Lane post office, conveniently situated for the tenants of Lincoln's Inn and the many offices surrounding it. Such convenience could not, of course, be allowed to continue, and in 1991 the post office (purpose-built in 1969!) was closed despite massive local protests including a petition to Downing Street, and relocated at the back of Rymans in High Holborn, several hundred yards away. No doubt the rent is cheaper, and the clerks of Chancery Lane will benefit from the additional exercise.

Continue north past Lincoln's Inn,

noting on its wall just opposite Cursitor Street the unofficial blue plaque erected by the Cromwell Association in memory of John Thurloe, secretary to Cromwell's Council of State (*not* Cromwell's 'secretary of state' as the plaque suggests).

At the top of the road we are back at the starting point of this walk.

Sources

Allibone, Jill & Evans, David. *The Inns of Court* Black Dog, 1996

Baker, J.H. *An introduction to English legal history* 3rd rev edn, Butterworth, 1990

Barron, Caroline M. *The parish of St Andrew Holborn* Diamond Trading Co., 1979

Barton, Nicholas. *The lost rivers of London,* rev. edn. Historical Publications, 1992

Bebbington, Gillian. *London street names* Batsford, 1972

Besant, Sir Walter. *London north of the Thames* A. & C. Black, 1911

Cherry, Bridget & Pevsner, Nikolaus. *The buildings of England. London, 4: North* Penguin, 1998

Colpi, Terri. *The Italian factor: the Italian community in Great Britain* Edinburgh: Mainstream, 1991

Davies, Rev. S. *The history of Ely Place* (pamphlet), 1920

Duke, N.E. & Campion, Bernard. *The story of Gray's Inn: an outline history* Gray's Inn, 1950

Department of the Environment. *List of buildings of special architectural or historical interest as at 14 May 1974 ,* London Borough of Camden DOE, 1974

Edwards, P.J. *History of London street improvements 1855–1867* LCC, 1889

Fairfield, S. *The streets of London: a dictionary of their names and their origins* Macmillan, 1983

Field Lane Foundation. *The Field Lane story.* 2nd edn. The Foundation, 1972

Forshaw, Alec & Bergström, Theo. *The markets of London* Penguin, 1989

Green, David. "The social economy of Little Italy in Victorian London" Unpublished MS, 1977

Hollingshead, John. *Ragged London in 1861* Everyman, 1986

Hurst, Sir Gerald. *A short history of Lincoln's Inn* Constable, 1946

Inwood, Stephen. *A history of London* Macmillan, 1998

Le Faye, Deirdre. *Medieval Camden* Camden History Society, 1975

Lehmann, John. *Holborn: an historical portrait of a London borough* Macmillan, 1970

Lillywhite, Bryant. *London signs* Allen & Unwin, 1972

Mackenzie, D (ed). *Holborn old and new* Princeton Press, for First Avenue Hotel, 1928

Marryat, H. & Broadbent, Una. *The romance of Hatton Garden* James Cornish, 1930

Megarry, Sir Robert. *An introduction to Lincoln's Inn,* 5th edn. Hon Society of Lincoln's Inn, 1997

Merriman, Nick (ed.) *The peopling of London* Museum of London, 1993

Norman, Philip. *London vanished & vanishing* A. & C. Black, 1905

Phillips, Hugh. *Mid-Georgian London* Collins, 1964

Richardson, W.C. *A history of the Inns of Court,* 1978

Roxburgh, Sir Ronald. *The origins of Lincoln's Inn* Cambridge U.P., 1963

Russell, G.W.E. *St Alban the Martyr, Holborn* George Allen, 1913

St Peter's Italian Church: visitors' guide* Pitkin, 1996

Stone, R. *Gray's Inn: a short history,* 1997

Stow, John. *The survey of London (1598)* Everyman, 1987

Strype, John. *A survey of the cities of London and Westminster,* 1720

Survey of London, Vol. 5: *St Giles-in-the-Fields (part II)* London County Council, 1914

Taylor, Gladys. *Old London gardens* Ian Henry, 1977

Thornbury, W. *Old and new London, chapters 57–62* Cassell, 1872

Trench, Richard. *London before the Blitz* Weidenfeld, 1989

Walford, E. *Old and new London* Alderman Press, 1986

Weinreb, Ben & Hibbert, Christopher (eds). *The London encyclopedia* Macmillan, 1992

Williams, E. *Early Holborn and the legal quarter of London* Sweet and Maxwell, 1927

Articles

Camden History Review: *Little Italy* vol 15, pp 2–6; K. Mansfield vol 8, pp 21–22; model dwellings vol 9, pp 4–9; WW II bomb damage vol 22, pp 11–15

Foster, D. *Alehouses etc.* [Westminster Archives]

Hunting, P. "The Survey of Hatton Garden" in *London Topographical Record,* vol.25, 1985

Pollock, F. "The origins of the Inns of Court" in *Law Quarterly Review* vol.48, 1932, pp 163–170

Simpson, A.W.B. "The early construction of the Inns of Court" in *Cambridge Law Journal* vol.28, 1970, pp 241–256.

Tyler, D. "Thomas Gainsborough's days in Hatton Garden" in *Gainsborough's House Review* 1992/3

Vitoria, M. "New Square, Lincoln's Inn and its flying freeholds" in *The Conveyancer and Property Lawyer,* vol.41 (new series), 1997, pp 11–17

Watson, Isobel. "James Hartnoll 1853–1900" in *Housing Happenings,* no.65, Christmas 1980

Other sources

Backhill (local Italian community magazine)
GRAYA (a magazine for and about Gray's Inn and its members)
Census records 1841–1891
Post Office London directories
LCC/GLC street lists

Maps, including Ogilby 1681; parish map 1720; Rocque 1746; Horwood 1799; early Ordnance Survey maps; Booth's poverty maps 1889–98; Goad insurance plans; LCC bomb damage maps; and Metropolitan Board of Works: metropolitan street improvements, 1: Holborn Town Hall to St John Street 1883

Camden History Society: photographic survey 1977–
Tallis, J. *London street views* 1838–40

Dictionary of national biography

Camden Local Studies & Archives Centre
Guildhall Library
London Metropolitan Archives
National Monuments Record
Westminster Archives

Index

Streets included in the survey are indicated in boldface, as are the main entries for these and other selected entries * = illustration